SEARS HOUSE DESIGNS
OF THE THIRTIES

SEARS HOUSE DESIGNS OF THE THIRTIES

Sears, Roebuck and Co.

DOVER PUBLICATIONS, INC.
Mineola, New York

Bibliographical Note

This Dover edition, first published in 2003, is an unabridged republication of the work originally published by Sears, Roebuck and Co., Chicago, Ill., in 1932 under the title *Homes of Today*.

Library of Congress Cataloging-in-Publication Data

Homes of today.
    Sears house designs of the thirties / Sears, Roebuck and Co.—Dover ed.
        p. cm.
    Originally published: Homes of today. Chicago, Ill. : Sears, Roebuck and Co., 1932.
    Includes index.
    ISBN 0-486-42994-6 (pbk.)
        1. Architecture, Domestic—United States—Designs and plans—Catalogs.
2. Sears, Roebuck and Company—Catalogs. I. Sears, Roebuck and Company.
II. Title.
NA7205.H668 2003
728'.37'09043—dc22

                                                            2003055517

Manufactured in the United States of America
Dover Publications, Inc., 31 East 2nd Street, Mineola, N.Y. 11501

Historic Mount Vernon Reproduced at Paris Exposition

In response to an invitation from President Doumergue, on behalf of the French government, the United States participated in an unique and fitting manner, in the French governmental Exposition Coloniale Internationale de Paris. The architectural plans for the American buildings carry as a feature a full size replica of Mount Vernon.

Following the approval of the architectural plans by President Hoover, the State Department decided that all materials and equipment should come from the United States—and awarded the contract for this and for the actual erection of the other American Exhibit buildings in Paris to the Home Construction Division of Sears, Roebuck and Co. These contracts were entered into the first part of October, 1930, with the understanding that all construction was to be completed by February 28, 1931. The confidence the United States government has placed in the Home Construction Division of Sears-Roebuck is merited by our well trained organization, which has built nearly 60,000 homes in all parts of the United States.

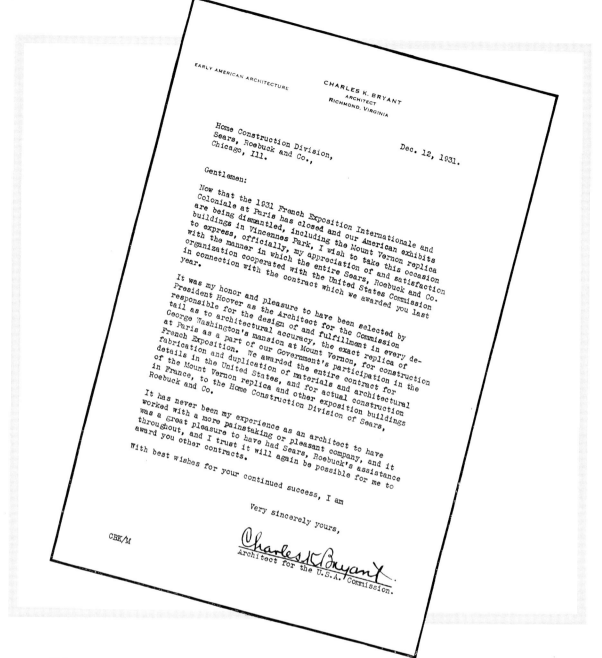

EARLY AMERICAN ARCHITECTURE

CHARLES K. BRYANT
ARCHITECT
RICHMOND, VIRGINIA

Home Construction Division,
Sears, Roebuck and Co.,
Chicago, Ill.

Dec. 12, 1931.

Gentlemen:

Now that the 1931 French Exposition Internationale and Coloniale at Paris has closed and our American exhibits are being dismantled, including the Mount Vernon replica buildings in Vincennes Park, I wish to take this occasion to express, officially, my appreciation of and satisfaction with the manner in which the entire Sears, Roebuck and Co. organization cooperated with the United States Commission in connection with the contract which we awarded you last year.

It was my honor and pleasure to have been selected by President Hoover as the Architect for the Commission responsible for the design of and fulfillment in every detail as to architectural accuracy, the exact replica of George Washington's mansion at Mount Vernon, for construction at Paris as a part of our Government's participation in the French Exposition. We awarded the entire contract for fabrication and duplication of materials and architectural details in the United States, and for actual construction of the Mount Vernon replica and other exposition buildings in France, to the Home Construction Division of Sears, Roebuck and Co.

It has never been my experience as an architect to have worked with a more painstaking or pleasant company, and it was a great pleasure to have had Sears, Roebuck's assistance throughout, and I trust it will again be possible for me to award you other contracts.

With best wishes for your continued success, I am

Very sincerely yours,

Charles K. Bryant
Architect for the U.S.A. Commission.

CBK/M

"If You Built *That,* I Want You to Build *My* Home"

We believe you will say this same thing as thousands of others have—after you have reviewed these beautiful homes and the details of Sears, Roebuck and Co.'s remarkable home building financing offer.

Just as Sears built in France a duplicate of George Washington's ideal Virginia home, so are Sears building in every type of community, homes of every size and style—the ideals of individuals in every walk of life.

These men and women will tell you that fine homes built under the Sears plan cost less than ordinary homes built under ordinary methods—and they will tell you that it takes less time and less worry to own your home the Sears-Roebuck way.

Now, it is your home that is to be built—your purse, your needs, your ideals of home ownership that are to be given every consideration. And we believe that when you have weighed the advantages of Sears unrivaled home building and financing services, after you have counseled with us, that you will make the same decision that nearly sixty thousand others have made, "I want Sears-Roebuck to build my home!"

The Largest
Home Building Organization
in the World

Everyone knows that Sears, Roebuck and Co. is in fact, as well as in name the World's Largest Store. Financiers, business and mercantile leaders can tell you that about one per cent of the nation's business—or about three hundred and fifty million dollars a year—is done by this one concern. No wonder! More than twelve million families are proud to tell you "We buy at Sears."

You should know this too. The Home Construction Division of Sears, Roebuck and Co. is the biggest home building organization on earth. It is a separate and distinct unit of the company, owning its own factories, employing upwards of 2,500 in its own organization, and with a trained personnel experienced, over 25 years, in every phase of fine home building. What other organization in the world can say the same?

Nearly sixty thousand homes already constructed—from foundation to roof—equivalent to the number of homes in a city of two or three hundred thousand people. In scores of cities there are complete construction offices devoted exclusively to selling these fine homes—modest cottages of four rooms—mansions of forty and more. Even exposition buildings for the United States Government! No building undertaking too large—none too small.

A giant craftsman. Fourteen million feet—about 70 times as much as the average yard is the storage capacity of his lumber plants. He operates ten great factories for building needs only. At one of them the huge ocean freighters come right up to his own docks to unload raw materials and supplies for this single forty-acre plant. That saves many dollars on transportation.

The enormous dirigible "Los Angeles" could conveniently find mooring space in one of the buildings at this Port Newark, New Jersey, plant if other equipment were removed. Nearly one hundred feet high, five hundred feet long, and one hundred sixty feet wide, this single building is a giant hive of industry itself. But there are others.

In Norwood, Ohio, the World's Biggest Home Builder operates a seventeen acre sash and door factory able to produce three and a half million dollars worth of millwork a year—doors, windows, everything that helps make four walls a home. And the eyes of the giant watch quality at every step. The best materials, skillful workmanship and low cost are his exacting demands of man and machine.

A birdseye view of our 17 acre sash and door factory in Norwood, Ohio.

YET ANOTHER 40-ACRE PLANT. To serve the great Midwest and South a combined lumber and millwork plant of forty acres is kept humming at Cairo, Illinois. Batteries of singing saws and crooning planers, creeping caterpillar tractors, and husky cranes are kept busy preparing material that will save the building workman's time and your money. If a special machine is needed to handle a job more efficiently, more economically, that machine is bought, invented, if necessary.

MACHINES DO EVERYTHING BUT THINK. Like mighty mechanical ants, and as busy, are the peculiar trucks that haul tons of building supplies *underneath* their stilt-wheeled bodies; fast moving electrically driven, they pick up their own piles and drop them down without a slip just as real ants carry crumbs.

One remarkable rafter machine does three things at once, beveling both ends and cutting the notch for the top plate with lightning speed, and absolute accuracy. Human hands cannot compete with such machines. Fewer minds are needed to guide them. But so great is the number of machines that hundreds of skilled mechanics are needed to operate those in our lumber and millwork factories alone.

ONE AND TWO STORY SKYSCRAPERS. Just as the big girders for the framework of skyscrapers are fabricated at the mills, so are the joists, sills, studs, plates, and rafters for your home measured, cut and marked at the factory. Carpenters like to have materials arrive this way, just as cooks like to have "butter the size of an egg, a cup and a half of sugar," etc., on hand when baking. Neither too much nor too little, but the right amount, of the right quality, ready to use. Furnishing the framing parts this way eliminates tiresome back breaking toil and enables carpenters to concentrate on construction, to work faster, do more and earn more.

CONTRACTORS PREFER THIS METHOD. Contractors recognize these advantages. One contractor who has built more than one hundred residences this way said recently, "Since there is no hand sawing to be done, and no waste of lumber, I do not have to charge for these. I pass these savings along to the home owner in the form of a lower construction price. This method is better for me too, because I can get the work done sooner and can send my men on to other jobs, handling more business in less time."

THE GREATEST VALUES FOR YOUR BUILDING DOLLARS. Our many lumber, millwork, paint and roofing factories, wall paper mills, and other related plants, reduce your building costs still further. When we build your home, we know what are the best materials and equipment to use, and the lowest price at which these can be obtained. Our tremendous buying power and our complete manufacturing facilities make it possible to obtain or produce these products for you at that low price. Only by buying direct from the World's Largest Home Building Organization can you make these big savings. Only from a general merchandise institution, such as Sears, Roebuck and Co. can you get an iron-clad guarantee of complete satisfaction. We are in the home building business to make life-long friends and to create steady customers for "The World's Largest Store." Nowhere else can you get such big values for your home building dollars.

What This Means to You!

First of all, doing things on a big scale implies tremendous buying power. Mass production plus this greater buying power means extra economies, prevention of waste, not skimping of materials. This in turn brings top quality at low prices.

But low prices aren't enough. The valuable experience gained by the Largest Home Building Organization in the World, twenty-five years of it, is worth much more to you. This twenty-five years experience saves you disappointment as well as money. It has shown the way, not only to lower home building cost, but to *better* homes, *better* construction, and happier home ownership.

•   •   •

Everything—
We Need to Build
—including Money!

PLANS. Here at your disposal to pore over and to study is the world's biggest library of fine home designs and suggestions. *Your* ideas and suggestions—what *you* want—are welcomed and made practical at a price you can easily afford.

Artists picture many fine homes for your study exactly as we have built them for others. Experienced home counselors confer with you so that you consider every comfort and convenience that will make your home most livable and attractive. Nothing is forgotten. Then the value of the completely built house is guaranteed as the final price to you. No needed "extras" later to "boost the bill."

Sears two hundred million dollar guarantee of satisfaction begins here.

MATERIALS AND EQUIPMENT. Only top quality materials and equipment with the best performance records, tested over a twenty-five year period in nearly sixty thousand homes. Only designs, patterns and colors most in demand by discriminating home seekers. No products less worthy—less desirable, deserve the backing of Sears unqualified guarantee. No unnecessary tax for heavily advertised

brand names. Sears-Roebuck fine homes, finely built, are their own publicity—in every community. And these complete materials, equipment, and appointments of your selection must give you just as much—in many cases more—satisfaction and service as you could rightfully expect from any similar products offered by any other concern in the world.

This is but one more way you are protected by Sears two hundred million dollar guarantee of satisfaction.

COMPLETE CONSTRUCTION. Sears-Roebuck employs the best building tradesmen in your community. Every construction detail from the breaking of ground to the final flick of the last paint brush is carefully checked by Sears engineers at each step of the way. This insures all workmanship meeting not only your local building code, and the requirements of the U. S. Bureau of Standards, but the higher, more advanced standards of Sears-Roebuck construction.

Again greater values are yours—guaranteed by the entire resources of this two hundred million dollar institution.

CONSULT YOUR OWN ARCHITECT FOR OTHER IDEAS AND ARCHITECTURAL SERVICE

SEARS BUILD FROM ANY PLANS YOU MAY HAVE OR PLANS PREPARED BY YOUR OWN ARCHITECT

Little or no cash needed . . low payments - monthly like rent

No. 1 15-Year Plan

If you own a well-located lot, for each dollar you invest Sears will lend you up to three dollars to build the house. You furnish one-fourth of the cost of your house and lot—Sears furnish as much as three-fourths. As the following examples show, little or no cash is needed to build this way and monthly payments are lower than rent for homes of equal value. Under this plan you can take as long as you want to pay for your home—up to fifteen years. No payments for the first four months.

Example A

Suppose your proposed home will cost........$4,000
And the appraised value of your lot is.......... 1,000
Total..... ....$5,000
Sears-Roebuck will lend you up to three-fourths. 3,750
Your cash investment in addition to lot would be only..$250
Monthly payments would be only $32.10.

Example B

If your proposed home will cost.............$15,000
And the appraised value of your lot is.......... 5,000
Total...................................$20,000
Sears-Roebuck will lend you up to three-fourths. 15,000
And your lot, therefore, is your only investment necessary.
Monthly payments would be only $128.40.

This plan means you can *stop paying rent* and apply that money to the purchase of a home! Ask yourself "How much money am I losing by not owning a home of my own?" You can easily figure it out from the following table.

Monthly Rent	Total Rent Paid in 7 Years	Total Rent Paid in 10 Years	Total Rent Paid in 15 Years
$ 25.00	$2,100.00	$ 3,000.00	$ 4,500.00
35.00	2,940.00	4,200.00	6,300.00
40.00	3,360.00	4,800.00	7,200.00
50.00	4,200.00	6,000.00	9,000.00
60.00	5,040.00	7,200.00	10,800.00
70.00	5,880.00	8,400.00	12,600.00
80.00	6,720.00	9,600.00	14,400.00
90.00	7,560.00	10,800.00	16,200.00
100.00	8,400.00	12,000.00	18,000.00

No. 2 5-Year Plan

We will lend you up to sixty-five per cent of the total value of the completed house and lot. Payments are one-half per cent of the principal monthly and interest at six per cent per annum. Home seekers who own well-located lots and who want loans for a short time only prefer this five-year plan. No monthly payments for the first four months.

No. 3 Farm Loan Plan

We will negotiate these loans to home seekers who own free and clear, well located, productive farm land; that is, farm lands not already mortgaged and which are self-supporting. In such cases we will loan up to fifty per cent of a fair valuation of the land owned. These loans run for not longer than five years. You pay one-tenth of the loan in the fall of each year and six per cent interest. Balance at end of fifth year. You may also pay oftener during the year or even monthly, if desired.

⋙⋘

How to Build Through Arrangement With a Building and Loan Association

Sears, Roebuck and Co. will ship the materials to you upon receipt of a letter from your Building and Loan Association, stating that the amount of our bill has been set aside for us and payment for the material will be remitted to us at certain periods as the work progresses. At your request we will be glad to furnish you the kind of a letter required by us, made out, ready for your Building and Loan Association to sign.

2% Discount for Cash With Order

We allow 2% discount if you enclose cash for the full amount—money order, draft, or personal check—with your order for a complete house.

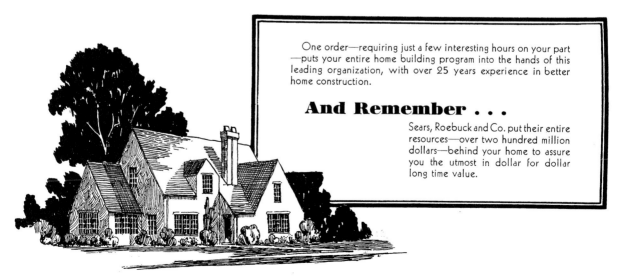

One order—requiring just a few interesting hours on your part —puts your entire home building program into the hands of this leading organization, with over 25 years experience in better home construction.

And Remember . . .

Sears, Roebuck and Co. put their entire resources—over two hundred million dollars—behind your home to assure you the utmost in dollar for dollar long time value.

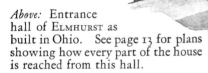

Above: Entrance hall of ELMHURST as built in Ohio. See page 13 for plans showing how every part of the house is reached from this hall.

Upper Right: Living room of the PENNSGROVE, which is described on page 61. The story and a half living room has panelled side walls and hewed oak ceiling beams.

Right: Living room of the LEXINGTON Colonial home shown on page 17, as it was built in central Pennsylvania.

Left: Living room of early American home built by Sears in Pennsylvania.

Above: An ELMHURST kitchen in Ohio. Gray, black, orange, and green make it most attractive.

Typical of Sears-Roebuck Homes

Above: Living room of eight room Dutch Colonial house built for a client in Pennsylvania. Your own ideas skillfully interpreted by Sears

Right: Two views of the 60 foot living room of the H-shaped early American home of log cabin style, built for Mr. and Mrs. Fuller M. Rothschild, Palatine, Ill. Vaulted ceiling and knotty pine walls.

Below: ELMHURST bathroom as built in Ohio. Equipment as designed by owner.

Above: A view of Rothschild's living room showing huge stone fireplace, bookshelves, lounging chairs and sofa. Ample light and ventilation in all Sears houses.

Right: One of the three large bedrooms in the Rothschild's home. Specially designed wardrobes and unique color schemes in all three.

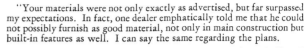

"I can truthfully recommend every dollar's worth of material I received from you people to be first class in every respect. Upon comparing prices I find that I saved over $1000 in buying my Oakdale home from Sears, Roebuck and I got better material. My heating plant simply can't be beat. I will gladly show anyone through my home who is interested and explain it to them."

WALTER BRUMITT,
Address furnished on request.

* * *

"I first want to express to you the splendid financial system that you people have. It places the prospective builder in a position to know from the start what his monthly payments will be and it is not like some financing companies, who will tell you after you have built what they will finance your property for. In other words, it gives you a guarantee instead of a promise.

"The materials that went into our home were very satisfactory and will say that I investigated very thoroughly all materials furnished by our local lumber yard and also by Sears, Roebuck and Co. before I bought and after our home was built. I have had numerous complimentary remarks regarding the lumber and its quality, also of the bathroom and lighting fixtures. The furnace is the best that I have ever used.

"Hundreds of people have complimented my wife and myself on the appearance and attractiveness of our home."

ROY G. WORNOM,
Address furnished on request.

* * *

"I have been in the building business more than forty years, and have built buildings and homes in several different states and most truly say that your building material in its many different lines is second to none. Your delivery is prompt, your terms liberal, and always most courteous and fair in your business transactions. Since using your materials, I figure that I have saved twenty per cent on each job—besides the satisfaction of receiving grades as specified."

J. W. BAILEY,
Address furnished on request.

* * *

"I have found that the plans for my Lewiston home were very clear and no trouble was met in carrying them out. The material which we received was of the finest quality and it was the cause of complete satisfaction. Upon comparing the cost of our home with that of other companies, I have come to the conclusion that by choosing as I did, a sum of approximately $1,600 has been saved. You have also my permission to have customers come and see my home. I will gladly take them through and point out to them the excellent quality of the materials, etc."

ISADOR CLOUTIER,
Address furnished on request.

"Your materials were not only exactly as advertised, but far surpassed my expectations. In fact, one dealer emphatically told me that he could not possibly furnish as good material, not only in main construction but built-in features as well. I can say the same regarding the plans.

I have given this building considerable thought—before I built and since—and have figured a saving of at least $1,000 over and above what the 'Maplewood' would have cost had it not been a completed 'Honor Bilt' house.

"The ready cut plan, to my way of thinking, is the only plan. The time saved alone in construction, is a very valuable asset and each and every piece fitted with such exactness that sawing was not even thought of. One neighbor remarked, 'It seems so strange—all the pounding and no sawing.'

"We are mighty proud of the 'Maplewood' home and can say nothing but words of praise of it and of the square dealing received from Sears, Roebuck and Co."

FRANK L. HITCHCOCK,
Address furnished on request.

"We shall always be glad to help anyone at any time in building their own home. We are so pleased about our Mitchell that we like to see others start their own home. It's so easy with your finance plan to back them.

"Judging from what other houses cost, I think I saved about $1,000. Of course, it is hard to get figures as the homes built locally are not completed by any means when the contracts are done. There are dozens of things still left to do then. I will have everything completed for $5,700, which I think is a great saving. The ready cut method is the quickest and I think the best, as it allows the owner to move in much sooner and so save about a month's rent or more."

JULES F. MOMMAERTZ,
Address furnished on request.

"It is with great pleasure that I take this opportunity of telling you about your wonderful service and quality of material used throughout.

I had a Lynnhaven Home built by your Milwaukee representative and I truthfully say that it is second to none anywhere you go. I take great pleasure in recommending Sears, Roebuck and Co. to all of my friends and associates. Courtesy and honest dealings seem to be their watchword."

HENRY J. MOLL,
Address furnished on request.

Sears Complete Home Building Plan

"I am very well impressed with the quality of the lumber that is furnished, and also with the generous dimensions of the lumber used for framing, especially for floor timbers, roof rafters, and ceiling joists; the very places some contractors usually specify lighter material. These things together with the good quality of workmanship going into the construction of our Lewiston home, has convinced me that a Sears, Roebuck 'Honor Bilt' home is a wise investment.

"You may direct prospective customers to our home and rest assured that I can, and will speak highly of your ready cut homes and your good financing plan.

"As to the probable saving that we made in dealing with Sears, Roebuck and Co., it would be hard to say, except that I have seen houses put up by local contractors that are no bigger, and certainly no better built, that have run $700 and $800 higher."

JOHN E. TOWNS,

Address furnished on request.

* * *

"The Sears Roebuck materials that went into our home were strictly first class in every respect and were favorably commented on by many people in the neighborhood who visited the house during construction.

"The local lumber dealer, who handled the material from the freight station, remarked that it has been a long time since he saw such fine material.

"Local builders state we could have built our home just as reasonable with local materials as with Sears Roebuck material, but all agreed they could not come up to the quality which you furnished.

"Your finance plan also is far better than any arrangement which could be made locally."

JOSEPH EBLE,

Address furnished on request.

"I am very proud of my Vallonia Honor Bilt home. The arrangement of all the rooms and wardrobes is ideal and much time and money was saved by the material being ready cut. I was well pleased with the superior quality of all the material which you sent and I figure that I saved about $1000 by buying from you. If I should ever build another home it would be an Honor Bilt."

DENCY ADAMS,

Address furnished on request.

* * *

"We will be glad to show any of your prospective customers our home and tell them how well pleased we are with your materials and service.

"We compared your construction with that of the local lumberman and found we were getting better construction for less money.

"They furnish only 2x4 rafters and ceiling joists, spaced 24 inches, while we have 2x6 spaced 16 inches—difference in thickness of flooring—paper under shingles—and a number of other things. We made good comparison before building."

IRVIN LICHTENWALTER,

Address furnished on request.

"The treatment I received from you in the purchase of my home and garage was so entirely satisfactory as to price, quality of material, mode of packing and shipping, prompt delivery, in fact in every particular, that if I should ever build another house or houses I would look nowhere else for the necessary material. I would not even ask for bids, but would simply and directly send you an order to ship everything needed and let the bill come with the goods. This much faith I have in you. Your guarantee really means something."

HENRY L. BRAMSTEDT,

Address furnished on request.

* * *

"We certainly feel well pleased and satisfied with our Bellwood home and the treatment and attention given us. Feel as though we saved money by getting our home through you and can gladly recommend Sears, Roebuck as being on the square, on the job, and wonderful to deal with.

"Have shown ten or fifteen couples through our home and feel as though, from their actions, they will buy from you."

THOMAS J. FREEMAN,

Address furnished on request.

* * *

"I have nothing but praise for Sears, Roebuck and Co. and their methods. Although I am not in a position to say how much money I saved on my 'Jeanette' house, I can say that I am satisfied that the material I bought from Sears could not be duplicated here, regardless of price. I am willing to recommend your Honor Bilt homes to anyone—and I have done so to many. Your system is good, your materials A1, your finance plan wonderful, and your entire organization is efficient and square in all methods."

RALEIGH R. MARTIN,

Address furnished on request.

Answers to Your Questions

reveal why Sears method is

AMERICA'S MOST POPULAR
HOME BUILDING PLAN

Do You Require Me to Build From One of the Plans in This Book?

No. Your home may be built from any suitable plans you already have, or from plans prepared by your own architect, in accordance with your own ideas.

Are There Any Advantages in Building From One of the Plans in This Book?

Yes, there are distinct advantages. When you build from one of these designs, you get a house that you know in advance is efficiently planned, and economical to build. With a few exceptions, each plan has been built several times and proved desirable from many viewpoints—as to size and arrangement of rooms, with regard to adequate lighting and ventilation, time saving construction methods have been worked out, and other improvements have been made.

Also, building your home from one of these plans is a sure way to get a home you can easily sell at any time, because only the designs most in demand are shown in this book.

Can a Sears-Roebuck Home Be Any Size, or Any Style?

Yes. There is no limit to the kind or price of home that Sears-Roebuck is able to build or furnish materials for. Any kind of home from a cottage valued at a few thousand dollars up to a forty room residence or larger, costing seventy-five thousand dollars or more. The home may be Colonial, English, Spanish, Norman or any other architectural style which the owner prefers, with exteriors of brick, stone, wood, stucco or other materials suitable to the design.

Can I Build Where I Want?

Yes. Sears-Roebuck homes are built in every size and type of community—in the residential districts of New York, Chicago, Detroit, Philadelphia and other metropolitan cities, as well as in smaller cities and towns.

How Much Cash Do I Need to Build?

Little or no cash is required. If your lot is fully paid for, or if you can buy one, its appraised value will be credited as part of your down payment. Your down payment need equal only one-fourth of the total valuation of both the lot and the house you build on it, so if the valuation of your lot is sufficient you need not invest any cash. In any event your cash down payment will be relatively small.

What Do Monthly Payments Amount to?

All the way from $25.00 a month and up depending on the value of the house. The designs illustrated in this book show the relatively low monthly payments which home seekers are called upon to make —payments that are less than the usual rent for houses of the same and even less value.

When Do Monthly Payments Start?

Not until four months (120 days) after you order your home.

How Long Can I Take to Pay for My Home?

You can have as long as you want—up to fifteen years.

Do I Have to Renew Mortgages?

No. Under our fifteen year plan there is no renewing of mortgages at any time. This is one of the most appreciated features of the Sears-Roebuck plan, especially by home owners who have experienced the worry and expense connected with the obtaining of new loans. When you buy your home from Sears-Roebuck you will not be saddled with unnecessary financing charges.

What Does Your Price Include?

Sears price includes full quantities of all materials and equipment necessary to make your home complete and ready to live in—window shades, linoleum on the kitchen floor, and in many cases, the electric refrigerator and other appointments you may wish to include.

In districts served by our Home Construction Offices, our price may, if you wish, also include the cost of complete construction of your home.

You know in advance exactly what you are going to get, and the price quoted is guaranteed as the final cost to you.

How Does Sears-Roebuck Handle the Construction?

In communities covered by field construction offices Sears-Roebuck engage the best building contractors and supervise all construction from start to finish. Materials and workmanship are tested and inspected each step of the way to insure meeting local building codes, as well as the requirements of the U. S. Bureau of Standards.

If you wish, you may engage your own contractor, in which case Sears-Roebuck will supervise the construction for you. In exceptional cases, where the owner is a contractor or a skilled building mechanic, he may do some of the building work himself under the direction of Sears supervising engineers, and the value of such work will be credited as a part of his down payment.

This constant supervision speeds up work and avoids material and labor liens, which so often cause expensive delays in home building.

The home owner is also assured of the best workmanship at the lowest costs, as the contractor knows he can rely upon Sears-Roebuck to pay him promptly and frequently for work well done, and he will not be forced, as he often is, to include in his price a hidden charge to cover the possible costs of borrowing money to meet his payroll.

If your home is to be built in a location not served by Sears Construction forces, we will cooperate in every possible way with your own contractor.

What Savings Can I Make by Building a Sears-Roebuck Home?

You pay less for materials and equipment. Sears, Roebuck and Co. own and operate their own plants and sell to you direct at very low prices. You save on construction costs, because much of the material of the house is quickly and economically cut by special machinery at the factory before being shipped, instead of being slowly and expensively cut by hand on the job.

You save on repairs and up-keep because of sound construction—and because the materials and equipment used have been tested and developed over a period of 25 years.

You save on financing. Sears, Roebuck and Co. provide the money so that you can build a home using the company's materials and equipment, and not for the purpose of making a profit on this money.

When you borrow building funds from a financial agency, their sole purpose, naturally, is to make a profit on the loan itself, and you must pay the customary fees, bonuses, commissions, and interest charges for use of the money.

How Much Time Must I Spend on My Building Program?

A few hours at the start is all that is required. One order placed with Sears-Roebuck takes care of everything after you have decided on your architectural plans—the materials, the equipment, and other services necessary to the completion of your home.

When you buy a home from Sears-Roebuck, one capable organization handles everything from start to finish, eliminating worry, trouble and loss of time on your part.

You place full and undivided responsibility in the hands of one reliable organization instead of the old unsatisfactory method of dividing this responsibility several ways.

It is unnecessary for you to buy your materials at one place, contract for building services somewhere else, and go to still a third source for financing (sometimes first, second and third mortgages).

Under the Sears-Roebuck plan you can order your home just as quickly as you can order an automobile, a radio or any piece of merchandise.

How Do I Know That I Will Be Satisfied With a Sears-Roebuck Home?

Because Sears-Roebuck guarantees complete satisfaction and because it is actually a great deal more important to Sears-Roebuck to see that this guarantee is lived up to than it is to you. The reason why is obvious. Sears, Roebuck and Co. is a general merchandise institution whose present large business was founded and developed on the well known guarantee of "Satisfaction or Your Money Back." The Company's continued success depends upon creating and holding the confidence and good will of millions of customers year after year.

The amount of merchandise which you buy from our Retail Stores and Mail Order Division, over a period of many years, will largely depend upon how well satisfied you are with your home, with its price and with the Company's services in connection with your building program.

When you buy your home from Sears, Roebuck and Co. you put the strongest safe-guard on your investment that you could possibly hope to secure. The Sears-Roebuck guarantee means exactly what it says and it is backed by the entire resources of the institution—more than 200 million dollars.

How Can I Get Complete Information and Prices on the Home I Want?

Just fill out the information blank in the back of this book and send to your nearest Home Construction Office or to Sears, Roebuck and Co., Home Construction Division, Chicago or Philadelphia.

The HILLSBORO

No. 3308—Already Cut and Fitted

Monthly Payments as Low as $55 to $70

THE EXTERIOR WALLS are planned to be finished with old English or tavern face brick, in colors ranging from light reds and browns, to dark blues and a few blacks. Cream colored stone settings give the exterior additional color and add strength to the appearance.

FLOOR PLAN. From the front terrace, we pass through an attractively designed batten type front door of clear white pine, with ornamental wrought iron hinges and hardware.

The hall contains a semi-open stairway to the second floor, which has wrought iron railing balusters and a small grille, opening from the stair landing into the living room. At the left you will find a passage through to the kitchen, cellar stairs and side entrance and lavatory.

In the center of the living room you will find an English design fireplace with built-in seat and bookcases at the left. The Tudor head plastered arch connects the living room and dining room to a small covered porch.

IN THE KITCHEN you will find a very compact arrangement, good cupboard equipment, built-in ironing board and convenient place for other equipment.

The successful designing of a garage as a part of the main building is desired

by every home owner but it seldom works out as successfully as in this plan. Garage is 12 feet by 20 feet, inside measurements, and provides additional room for work bench and storage.

The ELMHURST

No. 3300—Already Cut and Fitted

Monthly Payments $55 to $75

IN PRESENTING the Elmhurst design we do not hesitate in advising our prospective builders that this home contains convenient interior arrangement and exterior attractiveness, both of which can be secured at a minimum cost due to our time and labor saving ready-cut method of construction.

The main walls of the exterior are planned to be covered with face brick, while the gables are given an added touch of individuality by the use of half timber and stucco. The size, arrangement and design of the windows are such that they not only give plenty of light and air to the interior but also add to the well balanced exterior.

WE SUGGEST USING a brick which ranges in color from light to a dark red and also contains some browns and blacks. For the stucco, we suggest a light buff with dark brown trim members.

The floor plan contains living room, dining room, kitchen, breakfast room, lavatory, three bedrooms and bath.

FIRST FLOOR *has reception hall, living room, dining room, kitchen, breakfast room and lavatory.*

SECOND FLOOR *plans contain three bedrooms, bath and plenty of large closets.*

The WILLARD Five Rooms and Bath

No. 3265—Already Cut and Fitted

Monthly Payments as Low as $35 to $50

THE WILLARD is a two-story English cottage type of home and is a remarkable value due to careful planning and saving by our "Honor Bilt" system of construction. The Willard exterior has very attractive lines. The pro-

SECOND FLOOR PLAN

FIRST FLOOR PLAN

jection at the front, which forms the vestibule and closet, is very graceful in appearance. The exterior walls are covered with clear red cedar, gray prestained, 24-inch shingles, a very popular wall covering for this type of home. The front door is made of clear white pine of V-shape batten design and is decorated with a set of ornamental wrought iron hinges. The copper lantern over the front door is of English design.

LARGE LIVING ROOM, dining room and labor saving kitchen are located on the first floor—while two good sized bedrooms and bath open off the upstairs hall.

Fill out Information Blank, for complete details and delivered price will be sent by return mail.

The LAKECREST Five Rooms and Bath

No. 3333—Honor Bilt Homes
Monthly Payments as Low as $30 to $45

THIS STORY and a half bungalow type contains everything to be desired in an inexpensive home. Exterior attractiveness and practical interior arrangement. Note the graceful way the main roof curves down over the large front porch. The exterior walls are shown to be finished of wide bevel siding, but will look equally well in wide shingles stained a light color.

The first floor plan contains large living room, dining room and

kitchen. The location of the fireplace enables the kitchen flue to be carried in the same chimney. Two large bedrooms and bath open off the small hall at the top of the main stairs. Good wall space and plenty of light will be found in each bedroom.

No. 3333—Honor Bilt Home can be built on a 30-ft. lot. Fill out Information Blank for complete delivered price, copy of original architectural elevations and floor plans, and detailed specifications.

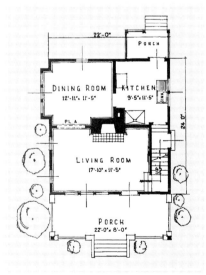

FIRST FLOOR PLAN

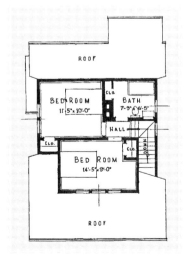

SECOND FLOOR PLAN

NOTE *that at the right, the open stair to the second floor forms a very definite division in the first floor plan. Arched doorways at either side make it easily accessible.*

PART *of the kitchen cabinet equipment was built out into the room to provide a recess for the cheerfully lighted breakfast nook, adding much to the convenient arrangement of that part of the house.*

THE CUSTOMER furnished the original rough sketches for this home and with architectural aid Sears, Roebuck and Co. built the English type house illustrated on this page.

THE EXTERIOR WALLS are covered with hard burned, variegated color common brick, with skintled mortar joints.

THE FLOOR PLAN contains living room, dining room, kitchen, breakfast room, bedroom, bath and two-car garage on the first floor with three bedrooms and two baths on the second floor. An interesting detail is that the living room floor level is two steps lower than the balance of the plan. This, together with the vaulted ceiling, gives this room a studio appearance.

Home of Mr. Jas. A. Bower, Anderson, Ind.

The LEXINGTON

No. 3255—Honor Bilt Modern Home—Already Cut and Fitted
Monthly Payments as Low as $65 to $80

THIS TWO-STORY RESIDENCE is an imposing and dignified study of modern Colonial architecture. The stately grandeur of this beautiful home is achieved by the use of wide siding for exterior wall covering, shuttered windows and an inviting front entrance. The attractive side porch adds a welcoming note of rest and comfort. Winking half fan lights flank each side of the tall fireplace chimney.

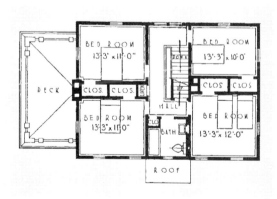

SECOND FLOOR PLAN

THE FLOOR PLAN comprises reception hall, living room, kitchen and lavatory on the first floor and four bedrooms and bath on the second floor, conveniently arranged around a central hall.

Fill out Information Blank for complete delivered price, copy of original architectural elevations and floor plans, and outline of specifications.

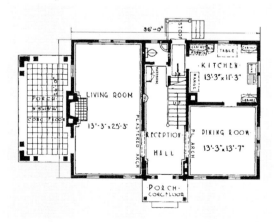

FIRST FLOOR PLAN

The COLCHESTER

No. 3292—Already Cut and Fitted
Monthly Payments as Low as $45 to $65

THE COLCHESTER is a modern English type which not only has beauty but an exceptionally well laid out floor plan as well.

In selecting the design, it is very desirable to have a home which gives a complete living arrangement on the first floor, to which additional rooms can be easily added at some future time. You will note from the floor plans that the first floor contains five rooms and bath, and that it is also possible to have two more bedrooms, with closets, and playroom or second bath on the second floor.

The motif or main detail of the front of this building is the happy combination of brick, stone and stucco. These materials have been given careful thought in designing the front entrance, fireplace chimney and

bay projection of the dining room. The size, design and arrangement of the windows, together with the broken roof lines, give this home a most pleasing appearance from every perspective.

THE LIVING ROOM and dining room are connected with wide plaster arch opening. These rooms are well lighted and contain exceptional wall space.

Three cabinets are a part of the complete labor-saving kitchen which also faces the front of the house. A small hall opening out of the living room gives the necessary privacy and connects the bedrooms, bath and stairs to the second floor. For copies of the original architectural elevations and floor plans and delivered price, fill out Information Blank.

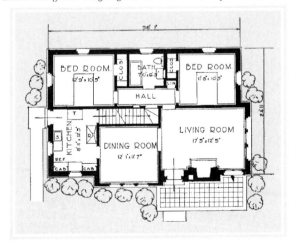

FIRST FLOOR PLAN

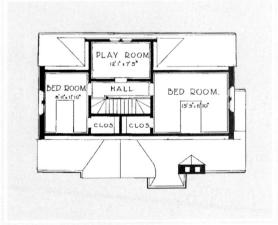

SECOND FLOOR PLAN

SEARS, ROEBUCK and CO.

The NEW HAVEN

No. 3338 — Eight Rooms and Two Baths
Fill Out Information Blank for Complete Delivered Price

This attractive Colonial home speaks for itself. It is that type that is always admired and its beauty lasts for years to come, on account of its simplicity.

At the left of the main hall you will find the vanity or powder room and lavatory, which saves ushering guests into the privacy of your bedrooms. That extra living room downstairs so often needed for library or den also opens off the main hall.

Note the step saving features of being able to go from the rear hall to kitchen, rear porch or front entrance.

Study the living room, dining room and kitchen and you will find good arrangement, lots of light and wall space. Large cabinets, latest type sink, range, table and refrigerator space have been provided. French doors open out to the decked roof of the porch making the hall light and airy.

Two baths, four bedrooms and eight closets use up every inch of floor space. What housewife ever has enough closet space—count them—eight.

Fill out information blank for architect's drawings and floor plans.

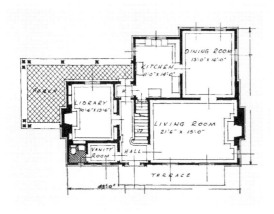

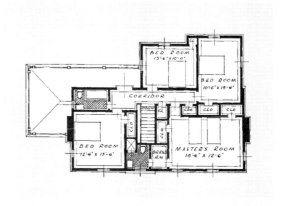

FIRST FLOOR PLAN

SECOND FLOOR PLAN

The DOVER Six Rooms and Bath
No. 3262—Already Cut and Fitted
Monthly Payments as Low as $40 to $65

THIS ENGLISH story and a half cottage has a convenient floor plan. The massive chimney, interesting roof lines, contrast of white or ivory walls with darker shutters and trim members give the house a smart appearance.

Hall. Opening off the central hall is a lavatory, an extra closet, and a stairway which can also be reached directly from the kitchen.

Extra Room on First Floor. This room with windows on two sides, and a closet, may serve as a bedroom, studio, office, nursery, music room or library.

Kitchen. Three large windows, top and bottom cupboard units, storage unit, and a built-in ironing board make the kitchen a pleasant workroom.

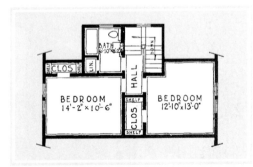

FIRST FLOOR—From the terrace, a circle head white pine door opens into a vestibule. Plastered arches connect vestibule, dining room and the living room.

Living Room and Dining Room. These rooms extend across the entire front of the house. Plenty of windows assure bright cheerful rooms and a pleasant outlook.

SECOND FLOOR—Two large bedrooms, each with two windows and a good sized closet. Notice the excellent location of the bathroom at the back of the house, near stairs and bedrooms. High grade bathroom fixtures. Venetian mirror and built-in medicine case, linen closet, and a built-in tub set into a corner, are other features.

The BERWYN Five Rooms and Bath

No. 3274—Already Cut and Fitted
Monthly Payments as Low as $30 to $40

IN DESIGNING small homes, the main thing to keep in mind is to obtain an attractive appearance on the exterior and a convenient arrangement of the interior and yet keep the construction cost as low as possible. In presenting this five-room design, we have observed the above requirements, resulting in a happy combination of these desirable features. The exterior looks equally attractive when finished with bevel siding or wide stained shingles. Under the front gable, a small entrance porch is designed, which gives the front door the necessary protection. The left side of the plan contains living room, dining room, kitchen, cellar stairs and platform for refrigerator. Two bedrooms, bath and closets make up the balance of this compact plan.

FLOOR PLAN
No. 3274—Honor Bilt Home can be built on a 30-ft. lot. For complete delivered price, fill out Information Blank enclosed.

LOOKS *Equally Attractive With Gray Stained Shingles*

The LORAIN

No. 3281—Already Cut and Fitted
Monthly Payments as Low as $35 to $50

AT FIRST GLANCE who would suppose that this charming Colonial house contained six rooms so large, comfortable and well balanced? Flower boxes and circle head dormer, repeating the lines of the gabled roof porch, lend grace to the Colonial simplicity of the design.

CAN BE BUILT

on a 30 foot lot. Fill out information blank for complete delivered price and specifications.

FIRST FLOOR PLAN

SECOND FLOOR PLAN

FIRST FLOOR—Living and Dining Rooms. Connected by a plastered arch, these two rooms occupy one entire side of the house. Entrance is from a porch with cement floor marked off to represent tile.

Kitchen, Bath, Bedroom, and enclosed stairway open from the hall. The kitchen has windows on two sides, a grade entrance, three attractively designed cupboard units, a broom closet, space for refrigerator near back door, and for stove near chimney.

SECOND FLOOR—Two windows in a back dormer light the stairs and the wide hall from which two bedrooms open. Each bedroom is over 14 feet long, with a closet, good wall space and liberal headroom.

The LYNNHAVEN Six Rooms and Bath

No. 3309—Already Cut and Fitted
Monthly Payments as Low as $50 to $65

WHAT picturesque possibilities can be hidden behind a few brick, stone, sacks of cement, a pile of lumber and millwork. It all depends on the design, but the result desired is a home with an attractive exterior and a conveniently arranged interior. All "Honor Bilt" homes are thoroughly tested to be sure that they contain these requirements which make happy, satisfied home builders.

In presenting the Lynnhaven, we feel that we are offering a home which will solve a problem for many home builders. The graceful way in which the front projection ties itself into the main building and the exceptionally attractive entrance, make this home one that will be admired by many. The exterior walls, covered with our Royal Red Cedar 24-inch shingles, when stained a light gray, give a very pleasing effect.

THE FLOOR PLAN contains vestibule, lavatory, reception hall, living room, dining room, breakfast alcove, kitchen, three bedrooms, bath and plenty of closets.

Fill out Information Blank and we will send you complete delivered price and copy of the original architectural elevations, floor plans and outline of specifications.

FIRST FLOOR PLAN   SECOND FLOOR PLAN

The MITCHELL Five Rooms and Bath
No. 3263—Honor Bilt Home—Already Cut and Fitted
Monthly Payments $40 to $55

THERE ARE SO MANY attractive details worked out in the exterior of this home that it would be hard to explain them all in this limited space. It is very evident, however, that the fireplace chimney, which is planned to be made of brick and stone, and the design of the front entrance and shingled side walls, which are laid with wide exposure, are among the most prominent features.

The door at the front is a batten type door equipped with wrought iron ornamental strap hinges. A very pleasing color scheme for the exterior is to use a light gray shingle stain for the side walls, with ivory trim paint for all outside finish members and sash; batten front door stained brown; shutters and small front window oxidized green, and color blend roof shingles.

THE VESTIBULE. The front door opens into a vestibule, at the right of which is a roomy closet convenient for placing outer wraps.

THE LIVING ROOM is 13 feet 3 inches by 17 feet 2 inches and is very well lighted by a triple sash window in the side wall. The plastered cove, cornice and carefully designed fireplace complete the outstanding features of this well planned room.

A double acting door is used in the opening between dining room and kitchen. Along the right wall, next to the cellar stairs, you will find a convenient place for the range and work table. The opposite wall is devoted to the kitchen cabinets and the kitchen sink. A mullion window placed high above the kitchen sink and a single window in the rear wall assures plenty of light for this room.

THE BEDROOMS, Bath and Closets are located on the right of the plan, the entrance to which is from the dining room through a small hall, which gives them the necessary privacy. Each bedroom has an exceptionally large closet and is well lighted. A good size linen closet is also designed to open off the hall.

FLOOR PLAN

The HARTFORD Four and Five Rooms

No. 3352-A—No. 3352-B Already Cut and Fitted. Honor Bilt Home
Monthly Payments as Low as $24 to $35

THE HARTFORD PLAN No. 3352-A contains four rooms and bath. Large combination living room and dining room opens from front vestibule. Kitchen provides ample space for all necessary equipment. The exterior walls are planned to be covered with 24-inch Red Cedar stained shingles. Note large, well arranged windows and graceful roof lines. Let us send you a copy of the original architectural elevations and floor plans.

No. 3352-B

PLAN No. 3352-A—*This four-room home is 22 ft. wide and 30 ft. long. Can be built on a lot 30 ft. wide.*

PLAN No. 3352-B—*This plan is 24 ft. wide by 34 ft. 6 in. long and requires a 30-ft. lot.*

No. 3352-A

THE HARTFORD No. 3352-B five-room plan contains well arranged living room, dining room and kitchen on the left side of the plan. Small rear hall also from entrance to cellar stairs. Large vestibule with closet for outer wraps is formed by the graceful gable on the front. Two bedrooms, bath and closet complete this plan which can be built at a very low cost. Get our complete delivered low price on all materials—by filling out Information Blank.

The MAPLEWOOD Six Rooms and Bath

No. 3302—Honor Bilt Home. Already Cut and Fitted
Monthly Payments as Low as $35 to $45

THE MAPLEWOOD is a story and a half English type in which the front gable projection and fireplace chimney form an important part. The exterior walls are planned to be covered with gray prestained wood shingles laid with a wide exposure to form a pleasing background for the dark colored shutters, roof and chimney. A batten type front door with ornamental iron strap hinges and English lantern above add considerable to the front elevation. The gable projection at the front forms the necessary protection for the front entrance and contains the vestibule. The opening from the vestibule to the living room is planned for a plastered arch in harmony with the openings between the living room and dining room and hall. This room is 16 ft. 3 in. wide by 11 ft. 2 in. deep—contains attractive fireplace, good wall space and three large windows. The rest of the front of the first floor is devoted to dining room, size 10 ft. 7 in. by 11 ft. 2 in.

A good size bedroom, bath and kitchen complete the first floor plan.

Two Large Bedrooms each with good closets open off the upstairs hall. A complete description of the guaranteed specifications for this home, together with a copy of the original ⅛ inch architectural drawings and complete delivered price on all materials will be sent on request. Requires a 35-ft. lot.

FIRST FLOOR

SECOND FLOOR

The SUNBURY
Four Rooms and Bath

Above—No. 3350 A Honor Bilt Home
Left—No. 3350 B Honor Bilt Home

THE FLOOR PLAN SHOWN BELOW
is designed for use with either house, No. 3350 A or 3350 B.

In the Sunbury we offer you the choice of two exteriors, with the same floor plan for either. With our modern methods the cost of the two houses is about the same. The house at the top of the page closely follows Colonial tradition, while the other is an American development of the famous Cotswold cottages of England. Both styles are in great favor and are sure of continued popularity through passing years.

The very modern floor plan affords four convenient uncrowded rooms, with bath, front and rear vestibules, four closets, breakfast nook, and a storage nook with shelves near the back door. The rooms are compactly arranged around a center hall and the ventilation throughout is extraordinarily good. A fireplace, linen closet, inside basement stair, and stove alcove, are some of the special features. A 38-foot lot is required.

Fill in Information Blank for complete delivered price and architectural drawings.

FLOOR PLAN 3350 A and B

The TORRINGTON No. 3355 Seven Rooms and Bath

BEAUTY in a home is not a matter of size or cost, for even the most compact and economical homes, if skillfully designed, can be lifted from the commonplace and given distinction which makes them a source of pride to the owner, and profit, should you ever desire to sell.

THIS BEAUTIFUL COLONIAL DESIGN is planned for a combination of siding and white-washed brick. It certainly will look dignified with dark green roof and shutters.

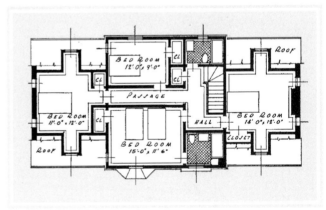

SECOND FLOOR PLAN

THE FLOOR PLANS are full of surprises because they contain everything desired in a home of this size. Seven closets, two bathrooms, first floor lavatory, four bedrooms, dining alcove, attached garage, living room, dining room and kitchen, all efficiently arranged with good wall space and lots of light.

It costs you nothing to get a photographic copy of the original architectural elevations and floor plans. Just fill out Information Blank and we will send complete prices and specifications as well.

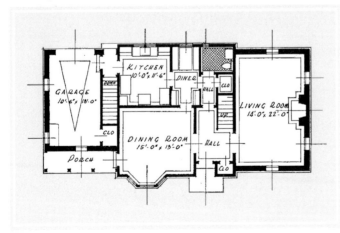

FIRST FLOOR PLAN

The JEFFERSON
No. 3349—Eight Rooms and Two Baths

DESIGNED along the same lines as historic Mt. Vernon, this southern colonial home spells success. Many types of colonial architecture have "stood up" for years with American home builders. Among these types the southern colonial has held its share of popularity and today is classed as one of the truest types. Exterior walls of whitewashed brick form a pleasing background for the dark green shutters and roof.

LIVING ROOM AND SUN ROOM, dining room and kitchen open off the center hall on the first floor. Note many convenient closets for outer wraps. Second floor plan contains hall, four large bedrooms and two baths. This roomy home boasts a total of ten closets.

Fill out Information Blank and we will send you complete delivered price, photographic architectural elevations and floor plans, also outline of specifications.

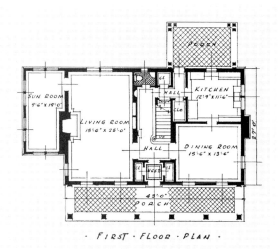

FIRST FLOOR PLAN

SECOND FLOOR PLAN

Designed by Mr. S. Merrill Clement, Jr., New York City

THIS BEAUTIFUL HOME is located near South Norwalk, Conn. Although the residence itself is on level ground, the approach, and also the land immediately above Mr. Spencer's home has a pronounced slope.

THE LEFT WING is devoted to a two-car attached garage with servants' quarters above. The main house contains living room, dining room, kitchen and three sleeping rooms.

The WHEATON Five Rooms and Bath
No. 3312—Already Cut and Fitted
Monthly Payments as Low as $35 to $45

INTERESTING roof lines are the order of the day from sky-scrapers to cozy bungalows like the WHEATON, the interior arrangement of which is as well planned as the exterior. Opening off the center hall are a model kitchen, a bath with clothes chute and medicine case, a linen closet and four comfortable corner rooms with cross ventilation. Front and back entrances are protected by vestibules and the amount of closet space is remarkable.

The house is 30 ft. by 37 ft., not including the kitchen porch, and can be built on a 40 foot lot. For outside walls we suggest our 24-inch Clear Royal Shingles stained gray and laid with 10-inch face. For contrast, paint the trim ivory and use dark brown for front door and Colonial shutters.

FLOOR PLAN: Through a vestibule 5 feet wide, you enter a living room 15 ft. 5 in. by 12 ft. 4 in. with plastered arches to hall and dining room. In three of the rooms windows are arranged in pairs for pleasant effect and inexpensive curtaining. The living room contains two such pairs of windows.

There are big advantages in a centrally located kitchen with side entrance. It saves many steps and gives greater quiet and privacy to the bedrooms. This kitchen contains built-in cabinets and storage unit, folding ironing board, sink near windows, and space for refrigerator in the vestibule. There is a 6-foot closet for each of the two large bedrooms.

Fill out Information Blank for complete delivered price together with copies of the original architectural elevations and floor plans; also outline of specifications.

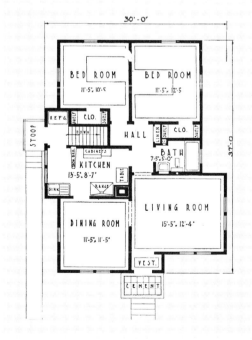

FLOOR PLAN

The OAK PARK Eight Rooms and Bath

No. 3288 Already Cut and Fitted
Monthly Payments as Low as $50 to $65

THERE IS A FASCINATING charm about this Dutch colonial home with its attractive colonial entrance. The front door is a six-panel design built of clear white pine. Glazed sidelights and fan shaped transom admit light to the front hall. The exterior walls are covered with 10-inch clear cypress siding, which when painted white or ivory form a good contrast with dark shutters and blended color roof.

FIRST FLOOR. A good size hall with a semi-open stairway to the second floor forms the entrance. The stair rail, treads and newels are of birch. The doorway to the kitchen passageway has a large plate mirror. The living room is 20 ft. 11 in. wide by 13 ft. 5 in. deep and the Dining Room is 14 ft. 5 in. by 12 ft. 11 in. with four sliding windows.

The floors of the dining room, living room and hall are of clear oak. Breakfast alcove and kitchen floors are covered with linoleum. The Kitchen contains two large cabinets and a broom closet. The back stairs form a space underneath the main stairs for the refrigerator.

SECOND FLOOR. By careful planning we have obtained four large well balanced bedrooms. The bedroom in the front at the right is 17 ft. 5 in. wide by 9 ft. 9 in. deep. Each bedroom contains large closets.

Fill out Information Blank for complete delivered price, photographic architectural elevations, floor plans and outline of specifications.

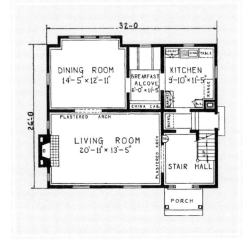

FIRST FLOOR PLAN

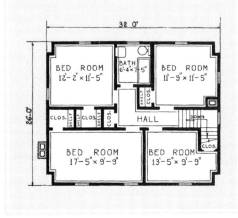

SECOND FLOOR PLAN

The CLIFTON Five or Seven Rooms and Bath
No. 3305—Already Cut and Fitted
Monthly Payments as Low as $40 to $50

BUNGALOW CONVENIENCE and two-story economy make the Clifton a beautiful practical and up-to-date home. The first floor is a complete five-room bungalow, but in addition there are two large bedrooms with closets and extra storage space on the second floor. The well-lighted corner room on the first floor may be used as a den, office, studio, nursery or sewing room, as desired.

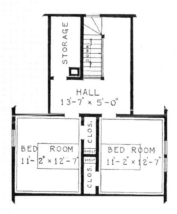

SECOND FLOOR PLAN

FIRST FLOOR PLAN

FIRST FLOOR. The living room has three windows and good spaces for furniture. A plastered arch leads to the dining room which has two windows placed together. A hall connects bath and two corner bedrooms, each of which has a large closet and windows on two sides. The kitchen is well arranged, with sink under windows next to the roomy cabinets, the stove in recess on the opposite wall, space for refrigerator with additional cabinets over and beside it.

Fill out Information Blank for complete delivered price, photographic architectural elevations and floor plans, also outline of specifications.

The STANFORD in Four and Five-Room Plans

No. 3354-A—3354-B—Already Cut and Fitted

Monthly Payments as Low as $28 to $38

THERE IS a certain softness of design and lasting character in the New England or Stanford type home. Many of the first to be built are still standing. With wide bevel siding painted white, and dark green shutters and roof, it is sure to make happy home owners.

PLAN No. 3354-A is size 30 ft. wide by 22 ft. deep and contains four well balanced rooms. Large living room and kitchen on the front and two bedrooms and bathroom at the back. This plan can be built on a 36-ft. lot.

PLAN No. 3354-B is 34 feet wide with five fine rooms and four generous closets. Large living room is 20 feet by 11 feet 5 in. A hall gives privacy to bedrooms and bath. Ample light, ventilation and good wall space are noteworthy features.

Fill out information blank for price and large drawings with floor plans.

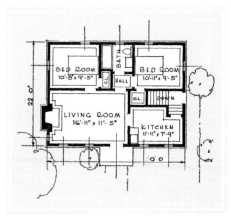

FLOOR PLAN No. 3354-A

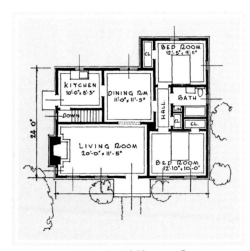

FLOOR PLAN No. 3354-B

The LEWISTON
No. 3287—Already Cut and Fitted
Monthly Payments as Low as $45 to $60

WHO would not take pride in being pointed out as the owner of this beautiful English home? There is a deep satisfaction in the possession of a home which truly expresses the good taste and the hospitality of the family, and a keen enjoyment in pleasant well proportioned rooms, arranged for gracious living.

The exterior combines stone and brick in the English manner, with leaded casements, long iron strap hinges, flower boxes, contrasting shutters and wood shingles laid with wide exposure.

The Lewiston is complete as a five-room bungalow, yet whenever needed, two additional rooms can be finished on the second floor, also a bathroom if desired, by placing a dormer in back. A music room can be arranged by making an opening between the living room and one of the bedrooms.

FIRST FLOOR. A clear white pine batten type circle head door leads

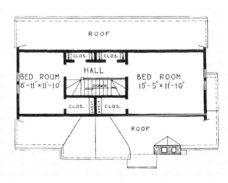

SECOND FLOOR PLAN

from the terrace to a living room with a fireplace flanked by leaded English casements. A plastered arch connects living and dining room, each of which has a group of three large windows. Good wall spaces for furniture in every room, and a pleasant outlook.

KITCHEN. With its cross ventilation, two large cupboards, sink near one of the windows and the convenient location of the basement stairs and rear door, one can work comfortably in this room while keeping an eye on outdoor activities.

BEDROOMS and BATH, also linen closet, phone cabinet and stair open off a hall which gives privacy to that part of the house. Each bedroom has cross ventilation and a good closet. The bathroom is 7 feet by 6 feet 5 inches with our high grade plumbing fixtures and Venetian glass medicine case.

SECOND FLOOR. At a small additional cost, two more bedrooms can be arranged on the second floor, also a bath and four closets. Two large windows on each gable end give these rooms light and air.

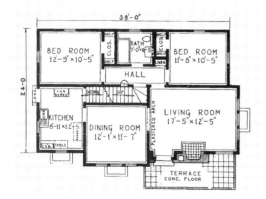

FIRST FLOOR PLAN

The WEXFORD

No. 3337-A—No. 3337-B—Honor Bilt Homes.   Already Cut and Fitted.
Monthly Payments as Low as $28 to $40

IF YOU ARE looking for something different in a bungalow design, you surely will find a pleasing exterior and convenient arrangement in the two plans of this Colonial Home.

PLAN No. 3337-A—HONOR BUILT HOME contains living room, two well lighted bedrooms, bath and kitchen. It really has five-room efficiency on account of the dining alcove recessed in the left wall of the kitchen. Combination grade and cellar entrance with refrigerator platform adds to this very compact plan.

PLAN No. 3337-B contains five well laid out rooms. Not a foot of waste space. You will find plenty of wall space—plenty of large windows and good closets. Both plans have a 14-ft. by 8-ft. porch with cement floor; a lot of added comfort when screened in the summer.

Let us send you a copy of the original ⅛-inch architectural drawings of the Wexford with outline specifications of complete materials furnished.

PLAN 3337-A
Can be built on 45-ft. lot.

PLAN 3337-B
Can be built on 50-ft. lot.

The JEANETTE
Honor Built Home—Already Cut and Fitted
No. 3283—4 Rooms, Bath and Dining Alcove . . . . No. 3283A—With Vestibule
Monthly Payments as Low as $30 to $40

THIS ATTRACTIVE little home is available in two floor plans. Although classed as a four-room home it has five-room efficiency. The front of the plan contains large living room, dining alcove, kitchen and rear hall containing refrigerator platform and cellar stairs. A small hall opening out of the living room gives the two bedrooms and bath the necessary privacy.

PLAN No. 3283-A is planned with vestibule added.

This feature can be had at a small additional cost.

Fill out Information Blank enclosed, and we will send you complete delivered price on all materials together with outline of specifications and copies of the original ⅛-inch architectural plans.

The quality and quantity of all materials used with Honor Bilt Homes is fully guaranteed.

The Jeanette requires a 45-ft. lot.

No. 3283A WITH VESTIBULE

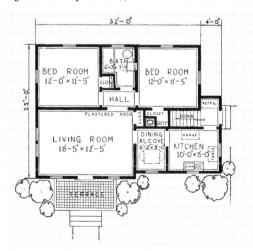

FLOOR PLAN No. 3283

The ROCHELLE Four Rooms and Bath

No. 3282—Honor Bilt Home. Already Cut and Fitted

Monthly Payments as Low as $25 to $35

THE FIRST thing you must consider in selecting a home is the size of the plan. Too large a home means a waste in investment, unnecessary work and expense in maintaining, and it costs more to furnish a larger house than a smaller one. By careful planning, it is possible to obtain an efficient, practical arrangement in a small design.

THE BUILDER of a small home is also desirous of having the exterior most modern and attractive. Americanized English architecture has been expressed in the lines of this home. Good window arrangement, with batten type shutters, solid White Pine batten front door and wood shingles for siding—all a few of the noticeable exterior details.

Every item of material that enters into the construction of this home is of the same high grade quality as is furnished in our larger types. The same proportion of saving is created by the fact that all the framework is cut to exact size, length and thickness at our factory.

THE PLAN contains a large living room, kitchen, two bedrooms and bath. The front gable forms vestibule and storage for outer wraps.

Fill out Information Blank for Complete delivered price, copy of original architectural elevations and floor plans, and outline of specifications.

Can be built on a 36-ft. lot.

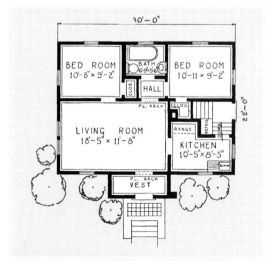

FLOOR PLAN

The STRATFORD

No. 3290—Honor Bilt Home. Already Cut and Fitted
Monthly Payments as Low as $50 to $65

THE STRATFORD is a very good example of a new type face brick bungalow that is fast becoming popular among the builders of small homes in this country. Due to the high pitched roof, casement sash, batten type front door and general rustic appearance of the exterior, it is classified as an Americanized English type bungalow.

There are so many attractive details worked out in the exterior of this home that it would be hard to give you a picture of them all in this limited amount of space. It is very evident, however, that the fireplace chimney, which is planned to be constructed of brick and stone with terra cotta flue pots at the top, and the front entrance are among the most prominent features.

The terrace at the front is planned to be made with cement, with the center colored and marked off to represent tile, and is given an additional tone of welcome by the use of an attractively designed bench used next to the fireplace chimney. The batten type front door is made of Clear White Pine and equipped with wrought iron ornamental strap hinges.

THE VESTIBULE. The front door opens into a vestibule at the right of which is a roomy closet convenient for placing outer wraps. This closet is lighted by a small casement sash shown in the front wall. The opening between the vestibule and the living room is planned for a circle head plastered arch.

THE LIVING ROOM. Size, 13 feet 2 inches wide by 17 feet 2 inches deep, is very well lighted by four full length French doors in the front wall and a single sliding sash window in the left. This room is designed to have a plastered cove cornice and also a very attractive fireplace. The recessed built-in bookcases on the left wall also add to the attractiveness of this room.

THE DINING ROOM. Size, 12 feet 2 inches by 11 feet 2 inches, is well lighted by a triple window in the side wall and contains very good wall space.

THE KITCHEN. Along the right wall you will find a convenient place for range and work table. The opposite wall is devoted to kitchen cabinets and a kitchen sink. The cabinets furnished consist of two top and bottom storage units together with a broom closet.

THE BEDROOMS. Opening off the dining room through a plastered arch, we enter into a small hall which connects the bedrooms and gives them the necessary privacy. Each bedroom has an exceptionally large closet and is well lighted.

Fill out Information Blank for complete delivered price, copy of architectural elevations and floor plan and outline of specifications.

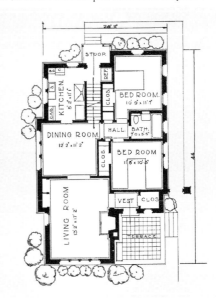

The JEWEL Five Rooms and Bath

No. 3310—Honor Bilt Home—Already Cut and Fitted

Monthly Payments as Low as $35 to $45

A FIVE-ROOM bungalow type design, probably the most popular of all American homes. In presenting this economical Honor Bilt home, the Jewel, we not only offer a compact five-room plan in which every foot of floor space has been used to the best advantage, but have also worked out an attractive exterior along the lines commonly known as Americanized English.

THE EXTERIOR walls of this home are planned to be covered with wide Clear Red Cedar shingles which are relieved of any suggestion of plainness, by the careful grouping of large, well placed windows with circle head batten type entrance door and shutters to match.

We suggest using light gray color for the walls with ivory or white trim and dark brown for the shutters and front door.

THE ENTRANCE from the front terrace is into the vestibule which gives the desired protection to the front entrance and offers a convenient place for hanging outer wraps.

The living room is 15 ft. 2 in. by 12 ft. 5 in. and is well lighted by three large windows in the front and side walls. Plastered arch opening used between this room and the dining room.

THE KITCHEN is sure to make many friends for it has a compact, practical arrangement for range, table, refrigerator, sink and cabinets, consisting of one counter and one wall unit.

Two well balanced bedrooms with large closets, bathroom and linen closet make up the balance of the plan.

Size of the Jewel is 38 ft. wide and 24 ft. deep. Can be built on a 45-ft. lot.

Fill out Information Blank for complete delivered price, copy of original architectural elevations and floor plans, and outline of specifications.

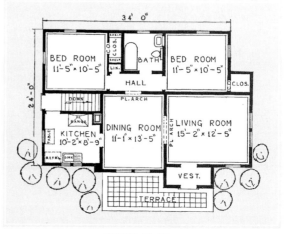

FLOOR PLAN

The CRAFTON Four, Five or Six Rooms and Bath

Nos. 3318A—3318C—3318D—Already Cut and Fitted—Standard Built Home
Monthly Payments as Low as $25 to $35

POPULARITY of this type home prompted us to illustrate it in three different sizes.

NO. 3318-C, size 24 ft. wide by 34 ft. 6 in. long contains living room, dining room, kitchen, two bedrooms, bath and good closets. The large front porch gives added comfort and can be screened in at small additional cost. Only the best materials are used in Sears Homes.

NO. 3318-D, size 26 ft. wide by 38 ft. long contains six rooms and bath. The front bedroom of this plan which opens off the living room can be converted into a den or sun parlor. The overhang of the eaves, graceful appearance of the front porch and proper window arrangement are features of the exterior.

PLAN 3318-A

NO. 3318-A, size 22 ft. by 30 ft. contains four rooms and bath, the feature being the large combination living room and dining room. The kitchen contains convenient wall space for all necessary fixtures. This plan requires a 30 ft. lot.

FILL IN INFORMATION BLANK and we will send you complete delivered price and copy of original architectural elevations and floor plans.

PLAN 3318-C

PLAN 3318-D

The BELLEWOOD Five Rooms and Bath

No. 3304—Honor Bilt Home—Already Cut and Fitted.
Monthly Payments As Low As $30 to $45

THE "BELLEWOOD" is another happy combination of a well laid out floor plan with a modern attractive exterior. The design is an adaptation of a small English cottage. Exterior walls are planned to be covered with gray pre-stained clear Red Cedar shingles, laid with 10-inch exposure.

The graceful manner in which the front gable roof curves over the vestibule gives this home an unusually inviting entrance. Careful grouping of the windows and batten type shutters also add to the exterior.

THE FLOOR PLAN. A clear White Pine batten type front door, equipped with ornamental wrought iron hinges, is used at the entrance to the vestibule which in turn connects with the living room with a plastered arch.

THE LIVING ROOM is 13 ft. 5 in. by 15 ft. 5 in. and lends itself to varied arrangements on account of good wall space. The balance of the left side of the plan is devoted to dining room, kitchen and rear hall with cellar stairs and refrigerator platform. Kitchen cabinets consist of one wall and one counter unit.

TWO LARGE BEDROOMS and bath complete the plan. The bath is planned to be equipped with Venetian mirrored medicine case and (Triple A-A-A) quality bath fixtures.

The Bellewood can be built on a 32-foot lot.

For complete delivered price, fill out Information Blank enclosed.

FLOOR PLAN

The WESTWOOD

No. 3299—Already Cut and Fitted

Monthly Payments as Low as $50 to $55

EXTERIOR. The Westwood is an unusual bungalow that is very practical because of its simplicity. This type home, without question has the maximum convenience at the minimum cost. The inset front porch is of practical size and gives the necessary protection to the front entrance. Large dormer, exposed fireplace chimney and good window arrangement are other noteworthy features of the exterior. The plan is 24 feet 11 inches wide, by 44 feet 11 inches in depth. Red or cream face brick of either smooth or wire cut texture will give the proper effect. All exterior wood trim members and moldings are furnished in cypress, which is the best material obtainable for the purpose.

INTERIOR. The left side of the plan is devoted to the living room, dining room and kitchen.

Located between the kitchen and dining room you will find the stairs leading to the attic which has sufficient headroom so that it can be finished off for two additional rooms if so desired.

The Kitchen contains convenient place for all fixtures such as range, sink, cabinets and refrigerator. It is equipped with one counter unit and two wall units.

BEDROOMS AND BATH. The right side of the plan is devoted to two large bedrooms with connecting bath. A small hall separates these rooms from the main part of the house. Each bedroom is well lighted by two large windows located to give cross ventilation and each has a good sized closet.

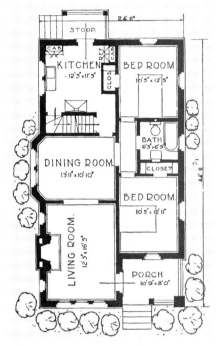

FLOOR PLAN

Can be built on a 35-foot lot

The NORWICH Seven Rooms and Bath

No. 3342—Modern Home

Monthly Payments as Low as $75 to $100

THIS attractive colonial home is the answer to many requests for a compact colonial type with attached garage. This picturesque home makes an instant appeal to all who see it. The architect has ingeniously utilized every bit of available space to provide seven rooms, bath, lavatory and two-car garage of ample proportions and at a comparatively low cost.

The exterior walls are planned to be covered with wide siding which when painted white or ivory forms a pleasing background for dark colored shutters and roof.

THE HOODED front entrance is well proportioned and gives the necessary protection to the front door.

The first floor plan contains living room, dining room, kitchen, pantry, lavatory and a second living room which is suitable for den or library. Note the attractive covered porch opening out of the living room.

THREE large bedrooms, seven closets, bath and stair hall complete the second floor plan. Plenty of large windows and good wall space are noticeable in every room.

In order that you will appreciate the real home value in the Norwich, we have prepared photographic copies of the original architectural elevation and floor plans. You may get a copy by filling out the Information Blank.

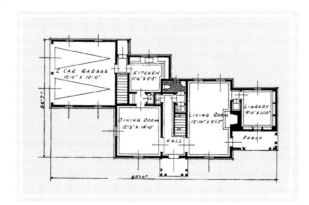

FIRST FLOOR PLAN

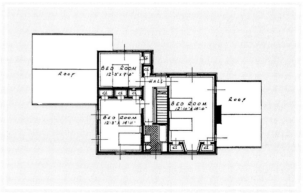

SECOND FLOOR PLAN

Page 44

SEARS, ROEBUCK and CO.

The DETROIT Five Rooms and Bath
No. 3336—Modern Home
Monthly Payments as Low as $45 to $60

A livable home with all rooms of the original plan on one floor—yet designed so that additional rooms can be added on the second floor.

The combination of face brick and siding used for exterior walls is especially pleasing. Clear White Pine batten type front door with ornamental hinges and wrought iron handle lock set is used at the front entrance.

From the vestibule entry which has closet for outer wraps, you step into the living room—a beautiful room size 12 ft. wide by 17 ft. 10 in. long with a lot of light. The dining room is also a cheerful spot with four large windows and good wall space. The kitchen is ideal in size and arrangement—just right for the housewife who appreciates a step-saving plan.

Note the location of the hall, which enables you to go from kitchen to bath.

The sleeping accommodations are comfortable in size and each room has cross ventilation. Two extra closets open off the hall for linen storage.

Fill out Information Blank and we will send you complete delivered price on all material, and a copy of the original architectural elevations and floor plans.

The Detroit can be built on a lot 32 feet wide.

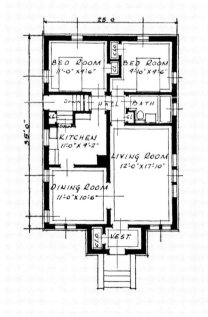

FLOOR PLAN

The STRATHMORE Six Rooms and Bath

No. 3306—Already Cut and Fitted
Monthly Payments as Low as $40 to $65

THE LURE of the old world charm and the luxury of the new world comfort are incorporated in this beautiful six-room bungalow. Never before has there been an opportunity to build a home of such distinction and quality at the low price made possible by our improved methods and facilities. Equal to the skill with which stucco, stone, brick and wide shingles are used in the English exterior, is the elegance and completeness of the interior appointments.

Stucco is planned to be used on the front wall between the left corner and chimney, and 24-inch shingles with wide exposure on the balance of the walls. The foundation is 34 feet wide in front and 28 feet wide in back. The length is 41 feet 9 inches, plus 6 feet 5 inches for the cement terrace. Six rooms, four closets, bath, extra lavatory, spacious vestibule and numerous built-in features are included.

Colors which will emphasize the protecting sweep of the roof as it shelters the entrance, and enhance the contrast which makes the exterior so effective, would be as follows: Buff stucco, cream stone, dark red and brown brick and gray wood shingles.

THE FRONT entrance from the terrace is into a large vestibule containing closet for outer wraps and forms the passageway to the living room, lavatory and front bedroom.

The living room is 20 feet 5 inches wide by 13 feet 7 inches deep and is well lighted by a balanced grouping of five windows and three casement sash above window seat. Every perspective of this room is good as to the proper size and placing of plaster arches, central fireplace, window seat with recessed bookcases and coved ceiling.

THE DINING ROOM is of ample size and has two large windows.

The kitchen is at the left where you will find an ideal arrangement which makes the duties in this part of the home a pleasure.

Broom closet, counter unit, two wall units and refrigerator occupy the space along the back wall with the front wall planned for sink, table and stove. The compactness of this plan, plus the high quality of material and our famous ready-cut method of construction, enable you to obtain a dignified attractive home at the lowest possible cost.

Fill out Information Blank for complete delivered price on all material, and a copy of the original architectural elevations and floor plans.

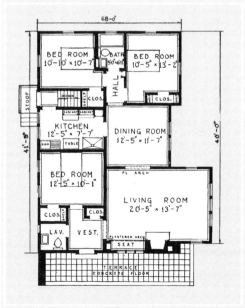

FLOOR PLAN

The BELMONT Six Rooms and Bath
No. 3345—Already Cut and Fitted
Monthly Payments as Low as $60 to $75

The first floor of the BELMONT home contains vestibule, lavatory, reception hall, living room, dining room, breakfast alcove, kitchen and under the main stairs a grade and cellar entrance combined, also refrigerator platform. All rooms have plenty of windows. The kitchen has four work units and the breakfast room has built-in table, benches and china closet.

A SEMI-OPEN stairway leads to an inside hall connecting bathroom and three bedrooms. The two large bedrooms are 15 feet 1 inch by 11 feet 11 inches and 15 feet 1 inch by 10 feet 11 inches. Four good size closets give plenty of storage space.

Fill out Information Blank for complete delivered price and architectural drawings.

THE BELMONT can be built on a 40-foot lot.

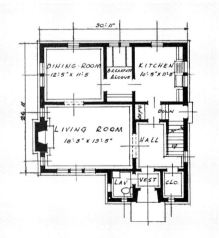

FIRST FLOOR PLAN

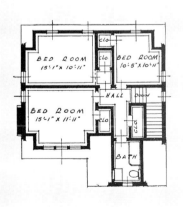

SECOND FLOOR PLAN

The MANSFIELD Six Rooms and Bath

No. 3296—Already Cut and Fitted
Monthly Payments as Low as $50 to $65

IN THIS English design story and a half face brick home, the entrance and chimney play an important part in the design. All exterior walls of this home are planned to be covered with face brick with the exception of the dormer at the rear which is of stucco, and the opening around the front door of which we have designed an attractive detail of stone work.

At the right of the front door you will find a large closet for outer wraps. A 15-light French door connects vestibule and living room.

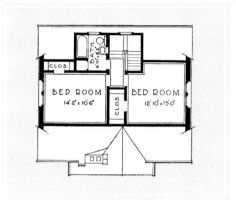

SECOND FLOOR PLAN

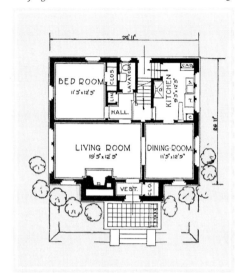

FIRST FLOOR PLAN

THE LIVING ROOM and Dining Room extend across the entire front of the plan so you can get a pleasing view from every angle. An attractively designed fireplace with wood mantel is located in the center of the front wall, and adds additional beauty to this part of the home.

THE KITCHEN. A built-in ironing board and convenient space for other kitchen equipment is also to be found.

THE HALL connects the lavatory and bedroom and also contains a small closet for linen and storage. The bedroom on this floor may also be used as a music room, studio, nursery, etc., provided a third bedroom is not necessary.

While the exterior of this home has the appearance of a one-story design, the roof construction is such that the two large bedrooms found on the second floor have very good head room.

SEARS, ROEBUCK and CO.

The WINONA Five or Six Rooms and Bath

No. 12010A—Five Rooms. No. 12010B—Six Rooms
Already Cut and Fitted
Monthly Payments as Low as $30 to $45

THE WINONA BUNGALOW is an American cottage type house. The vari-colored roof lines and cozy front porch give it a pleasing view from either perspective.

Plan "A" contains five rooms and is 24 feet wide by 36 feet long. Plan "B" is 24 feet wide by 40 feet and has six rooms. The outside walls are planned to be covered with 6-inch bevel siding.

Plan 12010 A—The vestibule contains a handy closet for outer wraps. The left side is devoted to living room, size 12 feet 6 inches by 12 feet 11 inches, dining room and kitchen. The kitchen is well lighted with two large windows and contains a good location for all equipment. Kitchen cabinets —one wall unit and one counter unit are furnished. There are two large bedrooms, bath and two closets.

Plan 12010B—Contains six rooms. Living room size 12 feet 5 inches by 14 feet 2 inches, and dining room 13 feet 11 inches by 12 feet 1 inch. Kitchen contains three large windows, one counter unit and one wall unit, and additional cabinet space built in above refrigerator which opens on to back hall. Each bedroom has two windows and a good sized closet.

Fill out Information Blank for price and for architectural drawings.

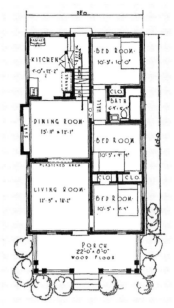

FLOOR PLAN No. 12010-B

FLOOR PLAN No. 12010-A

The BROOKWOOD Six Rooms and Bath

No. 3303—Already Cut and Fitted

Monthly Payments as Low as $40 to $50

The Brookwood contains the maximum livable floor area in a plan, 26 feet wide by 22 feet deep, a happy attractive exterior and can be obtained at a low cost.

The exterior walls are planned to be covered with 24-inch red cedar gray stained shingles laid with wide exposure. This home has a very attractive perspective from either view, due to careful window arrangement, colonial shutters and well balanced roof lines.

FROM the front cement terrace you enter the vestibule which contains a large closet on the left side for outer wraps. The living room is 12 feet 5 inches wide by 17 feet 8 inches deep and contains a large triple window in the center of the left wall. The openings between the living room and vestibule, dining room and stairs are planned for circle head plastered arches. The good wall space will permit a varied arrangement of furniture.

SECOND FLOOR PLAN

To the right of the living room you enter the dining room, size 12 feet 5 inches by 11 feet 3 inches, which is lighted by three large sliding windows.

THE KITCHEN contains a convenient place for all necessary fixtures and equipment. The rear entrance is formed by a combination grade and cellar stairs, also contains a platform suitable for refrigerator.

The small hall at the top of the main stairs connects the three bed rooms and bath.

THE LEFT front bedroom is 12 feet 3 inches by 9 feet, contains a double sliding window in the side wall and gets cross ventilation from the small window located in the front closet. The other two bedrooms are 12 feet 5 inches by 10 feet 2 inches and 12 feet 5 inches by 10 feet 8 inches, with good closets, cross ventilation and good wall spaces.

Fill out Information Blank for complete delivered price on all material and copy of the original architectural elevations and floor plans.

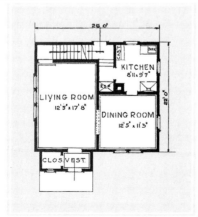

FIRST FLOOR PLAN

The COLLINGWOOD Five Rooms and Bath

No. 3280—Already Cut and Fitted

Monthly Payments as Low as $40 to $50

Here is an unusual bungalow, well suited for modern living conditions. The exterior is very practical and finds much favor on account of its simplicity. The lines of the hip roof are broken by the dormer on the front and bay projection over the dining room at the side. Living out of doors, as most of us do in summer, the front porch will be appreciated. The windows are very well designed and attractively arranged.

THE LIVING ROOM. From the front porch we enter the living room, which is 12 ft. 9 in. wide by 18 ft. 5 in. deep. A convenient and attractively designed fireplace in the left wall, on each side of which is a casement window, and a triple window in the front wall.

THE DINING ROOM. The dining room is located next to the living room at the rear and is lighted by two large windows contained in the bay projection.

THE KITCHEN. From the dining room we pass into the kitchen, where considerable thought has been given to the placing of many built-in features and practical arrangement of other equipment. The kitchen sink is located underneath the double window on the left wall, on each side of which we furnish suitable kitchen cabinets. A place for brooms, mops, etc., is formed by the closet opening off the right wall. The built-in breakfast alcove occupies the space at the rear.

BEDROOMS. A plastered arched opening is used in the opening between the dining room and hall which connects the two bedrooms and bath.

Fill out Information Blank for complete delivered price on all material and a copy of the architectural drawings. The Collingwood can be built on a 32-foot lot.

FLOOR PLAN

The CARROLL Seven Rooms and Bath

No. 3344—Modern Home

Monthly Payments as Low as $65 to $80

THE VALUE in this plan has been studied by six prominent house architects who all voted it a success. A successful plan is one that gives the home owner convenience, beauty and comfort at the minimum cost.

Study the floor plans of the Carroll and you will have to agree that it contains the maximum livable floor area and no waste space.

The front entrance, which is located so that the house can be placed on a wide or narrow lot, opens into a vestibule which contains small closet for outer wraps. To the right side of the vestibule are the living room and sun parlor, which when combined, form a room about 28 feet long by 14 feet deep. An attractive fireplace, plenty of windows and good wall space will be found. From the left of the vestibule the dining room and adjoining kitchen are reached. The kitchen is entirely out of sight from the front rooms. A rear hall contains entrance to basement and refrigerator nook. Five closets, three bedrooms and well arranged bath complete the second floor plan.

Fill out Information Blank and we will send you complete delivered price on all material and a copy of the original architectural elevations and floor plans.

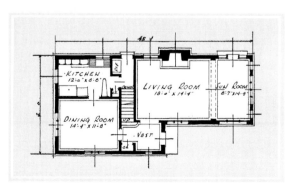

FIRST FLOOR PLAN

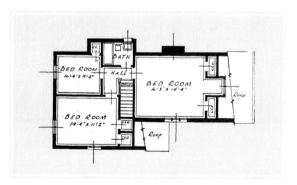

SECOND FLOOR PLAN

SEARS, ROEBUCK and CO.

The BIRMINGHAM Eight Rooms and Bath

No. 3332—Modern Home
Monthly Payments as Low as $50 to $75

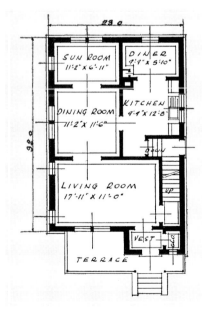

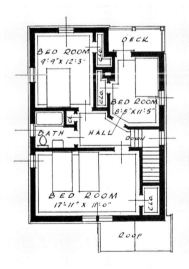

The BIRMINGHAM is a two story house designed for a narrow city lot, but skillfully given the appearance of a handsome bungalow, having face brick walls, and ornamental iron railing on a cement terrace.

FIRST FLOOR has vestibule and closet, living, dining, and sun room, kitchen and alcove.

SECOND FLOOR includes three large bedrooms, bath, four closets and a convenient rear airing porch.

Fill out Information Blank for price and drawings.

The ELLSWORTH Four Rooms and Bath

No. 3341 Honor Bilt Home

Among houses of commonplace appearance, even though they be much more expensive, the Ellsworth four-room bungalow stands out as a shining example of good architecture. Inside and out it has simplicity, charm, and completeness seldom found in houses of such moderate size and cost. Shingle siding, shutters, and shadows give the walls a soft texture, while the massive chimney and interesting roof offer a good skyline. A 38-foot lot is required.

From the shelter of a porch under the main roof, you enter an 18-foot living room with center fireplace, three large windows and good wall spaces. A bath at the back, and two 12-foot bedrooms each with closet and cross ventilation, are connected by a hall containing a coat closet. Linen closet in bathroom.

A delightful breakfast nook with windows on two sides opens off an uncrowded kitchen having built-in cabinets, recess for stove, broom closet, and double drain board sink under two windows. An inside basement stair with a storage nook helps keep the kitchen clean and comfortable in all weather. Ventilation throughout the house is excellent. Fill out Information Blank for complete delivered price and architectural drawings.

FLOOR PLAN

The DEXTER Ten Room Income Home

No. 3331—Modern Home
Monthly Payments as Low as $75 to $100

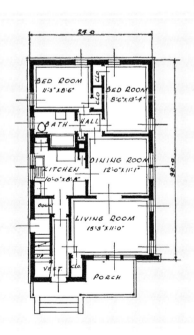

FIRST FLOOR PLAN

The DEXTER "Income Bungalow" looks like a handsome single family residence, but actually contains two complete five-room apartments. Rental income from one apartment greatly reduces the owner's payments and may in time pay for the entire building. Good design happily combines face brick, stucco, and stained shingles. The house is 24 ft. by 38 ft. and fits a 30 foot lot. Ornamental iron railing encloses the cement terrace.

FLOOR PLANS: Each apartment has a centrally located kitchen and two bedrooms with cross ventilation and closets. A hall with linen closet gives privacy to bath and bedrooms. Coat closet, kitchen cabinets and recessed bath tub are other good features.

One reception hall gives both families access to the side entrance or basement, thereby saving steps, reducing building costs, and affording larger and more pleasant rooms. Grouped windows in living rooms, dining rooms, and kitchens are attractive and can be more economically curtained. Good wall spaces in all rooms.

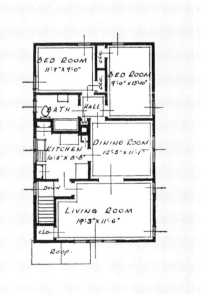

SECOND FLOOR PLAN

Fill out Information Blank for complete price and copy of architect's drawings and floor plans.

The CORNING Seven Rooms and Three Baths
With Dining Alcove and Attached Garage
No. 3357 Honor Bilt Home

FIRST FLOOR PLAN

SECOND FLOOR PLAN

The Corning, with dormers cut into the eaves, interesting door detail, and a dozen delightful points of departure from other Colonial styles, suggests old time Maryland.

But it is a far cry from the rambling houses of those leisurely times to the efficient floor plan here shown. Tucked in with the seven rooms are two complete baths, a toilet with shower, and an extra first floor toilet. Add twelve closets, a breakfast room, halls, vestibules, four entrances, front and back stairs, and an attached double garage and it is seen that the Corning is very modern indeed.

From the 22½-foot living room with bookcases, fireplace, and grouped windows, French doors lead to a porch of room size. Built-in cabinets fill one wall of the breakfast room and much of the kitchen wall space. Bay windows lend charm to dining and breakfast rooms.

Upstairs are four large pleasant rooms with excellent ventilation, two complete baths and one shower room with toilet. Liberal closet space throughout the house. Two double wardrobes are provided for the largest bedroom.

Fill in Information Blank for complete delivered price and architectural drawings.

The TRENTON Seven Rooms and Three Baths

With Dining Alcove and Attached Garage

No. 3351 Honor Bilt Home

In the TRENTON a graceful roof line over a trim exterior tells its own tale of quiet good taste and pleasant living. Spacious, airy, well arranged rooms with unusual built-in features, afford utmost comfort.

Living, dining, and breakfast rooms face the garden, likewise all three upstairs bedrooms. Service entrance connects with garage or any part of house. Fireplace, bookcases, wide window seat, concave china closet, numerous modern cabinets, six other closets, and an additional bedroom with bath, offer convenience throughout the first floor. The living room, with windows on three sides, is reached through a deep arch from the dignified stair hall.

On the second floor, three large bedrooms with another seven closets and two bathrooms, are connected by a well lighted hall. Deep window seats are also found in two of these bedrooms.

Fill out the Information Blank for complete delivered price and a copy of the original architectural elevations and floor plans.

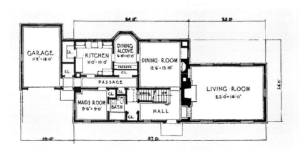

FIRST FLOOR PLAN

SECOND FLOOR PLAN

The CARRINGTON Seven Rooms, Two Baths

No. 3353—Modern Home

Monthly Payments as Low as $75 to $100

The CARRINGTON derives its individuality and charm from the Colonial houses of Salem, having overhung second story. The stone finish of the first story front wall adds strength and color, and ties in nicely with the stone chimney and siding. A large dining room bay and wide terrace in back make the garden but an outdoor room.

FIRST FLOOR: A hall 8 ft. wide with Colonial stair, two closets and lavatory, connects all rooms and terrace.

Notice large size of rooms and the step saving position of the kitchen with its side entrance. A fireplace and built-in features in every room add beauty and comfort.

SECOND FLOOR: Four large light bedrooms open off a wide hall, also one bath and a linen closet. The other bath and two of the seven closets, open off the large bedroom which overlooks the garden. Send in Information Blank for complete delivered price on all materials and large copies of architects' drawings with floor plans.

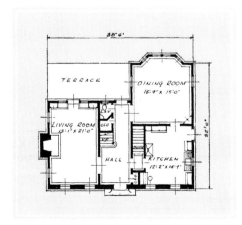

FIRST FLOOR PLAN

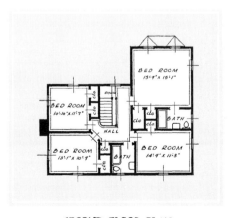

SECOND FLOOR PLAN

S E A R S ,   R O E B U C K   a n d   C O .

The KENFIELD Seven Rooms and Bath
No. 3343 Modern Home
Monthly Payments as Low as $75 to $100

From every viewpoint, the KENFIELD reveals the charm of those lovely old Maryland homes which seem literally tied to the ground by ramblers and hollyhocks. Large sunny rooms and numerous conveniences fulfill all the fair promises of the exterior.

A few of the unusual features are the coat closet, lavatory and beautiful bedroom reached through the front hall; the kitchen from which front or back door can be

SECOND FLOOR PLAN

reached in a step or two; the nine closets; and such built-in features as fireplace, two window seats, kitchen cabinets, Colonial china cabinet, broom closet, sleeping porch, and garden porch adjoining the living and dining rooms. The rooms are of more than average size with large windows and good wall space.

Fill out Information Blank and we will send you complete delivered price on all material and a copy of the large architectural drawings and floor plans.

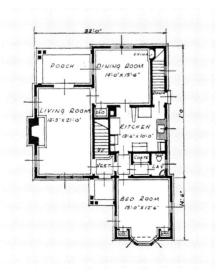

FIRST FLOOR PLAN

The GLADSTONE Six Rooms and Bath

No. 3315A—3315B—Already Cut and Fitted
Monthly Payments as Low as $40 to $55

PLAN 3315-B. First Floor: Those who desire a front vestibule and a stair hall will prefer plan 3315-B, in which living and dining room are on the right connected by a plastered arch; and the kitchen is on the left within direct reach of front hall. In this excellent arrangement, there is a combined kitchen and basement entrance at the side with space for refrigerator and door to front hall.

SECOND FLOOR: Three bedrooms, linen closet and well arranged bath open off a small hall. Each bedroom has a closet and two or three windows.

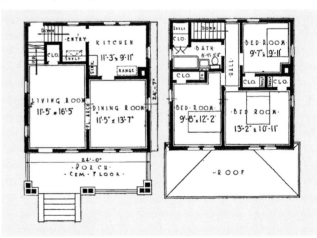

FIRST FLOOR—No. 3315-A   SECOND FLOOR—No. 3315-A

PLAN 3315-A. First Floor. Those who appreciate having both living and dining rooms at the front and who like the kitchen door in back, will prefer plan 3315-A. The living room is 11 ft. 5 in. by 16 ft. 5 in., with three windows and mirror door coat closet. A door at grade level serves kitchen and basement.

SECOND FLOOR: Bath and three bedrooms open off a straight hall with a window at one end. Each bedroom has a closet and two or more windows. A large storage or linen closet opens from the bathroom. Fill out Information Blank for complete delivered price.

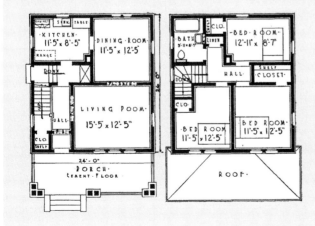

FIRST FLOOR—No. 3315-B   SECOND FLOOR—No. 3315-B

The LA SALLE Nine Rooms, Two Baths for Two Families

No. 3243—Already Cut and Fitted

Monthly Payments as Low as $45 to $60

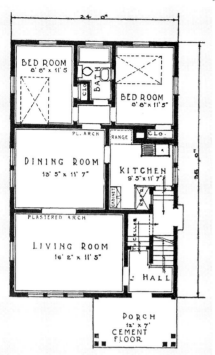

FIRST FLOOR PLAN

The LA SALLE appears to be a handsome Colonial one-family home, but contains two complete apartments. The rental goes far toward paying the cost of the building. It could easily be made into an eight room house with two baths at any time.

FIRST FLOOR: One reception hall gives both families direct access to side entrance or basement. Living room is over 16 ft. long with an archway to dining room. A hall connects bath and two bedrooms, each of which has a closet and cross ventilation. The centrally placed kitchen saves steps.

SECOND FLOOR: A hall connects all rooms. Off the living room is a big closet suitable for wall bed if needed. A large room with four windows is divided by china cabinets into dining room and kitchen. The larger bedroom permits use of twin beds. China cases, kitchen cabinets and four closets are included.

Fill in Information Blank for complete delivered price and large architectural drawings with floor plans.

SECOND FLOOR PLAN

The RANDOLPH Five Rooms and Bath

No. 3297—Already Cut and Fitted

Monthly Payments as Low as $45 to $60

Very attractive is the RANDOLPH with its brick walls, dormers, tall chimney and front gable of stucco and rough sawed siding. We suggest rough textured face brick from light red to dark brown and a few blacks, contrasted with cream colored stucco and dark brown stain for gable siding and timbers.

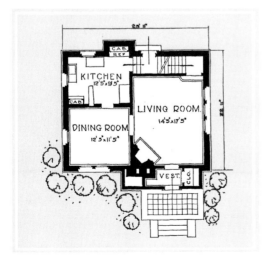

FIRST FLOOR: A plaster arch connects living and dining rooms, each having three windows. Notice the pretty Colonial mantel in one corner, also the vestibule closet. The light, convenient and well ventilated kitchen contains cabinets, refrigerator nook, built-in ironing board, and a grade entrance.

SECOND FLOOR: Off the hall are bath, linen closet and two bedrooms, each having two or more windows and a closet. The larger bedroom is over 14 ft. long with a big closet. Fill out Information Blank for price and large drawings with floor plans.

The ROXBURY Five Rooms and Bath
No. 3340—Modern Home
Monthly Payments as Low as $40 to $55

MORE popular than ever, are five room brick bungalows like the "Roxbury," which is a particularly good example of Americanized English architecture and of compact convenience. The walls of face brick in blended tones, are further beautified by careful grouping of windows, by the circle head entrance and stained shingles in the gables. FLOOR PLAN: The living room is protected by a vestibule, size 8 ft. by 3 ft. 6 in. which offers a convenient place for hanging outer wraps.

Note the good wall space in the living room which is 15 ft. 2 in. by 12 ft. 5 in., and is well lighted by three large windows in the front and side wall. The opening between the living room and dining room is planned for a plastered circle head arch, which is also used in the opening between the dining room and hall. The dining room is 11 ft. 1 in., by 13 ft. 5 in., and the openings are such that you will find a convenient place for all furniture.

In the homes of our grandparents, a large kitchen was essential, but in the present day the most popular kitchen is one that has a compact arrangement and saves steps for the housewife. The kitchen in the Roxbury is sure to make many friends, for it has a practical arrangement for range, table, refrigerator, sink and cabinets. A small hall back of the kitchen forms a side entrance and a landing for the cellar stairs.

CONNECTING HALL gives the necessary privacy to the bedrooms and bath, each bedroom being 11 ft. 5 in.

by 10 ft. 5 in. with good closet space. An additional closet for linens opens off the hall. The bathroom is above the average for a home of this size and contains a built-in medicine case, as well as our standard high grade plumbing fixtures. The size of the plan is 38 feet 10 in. wide by 24 ft. 10 in. in depth.

Fill out Information Blank for complete delivered price on material and a copy of the drawings and floor plans.

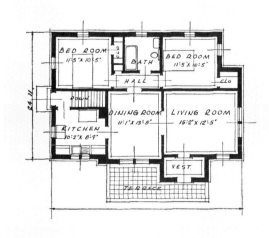

FLOOR PLAN

The RICHMOND Six Rooms and Bath

No. 3360 Honor Bilt Home

The RICHMOND, reminiscent of the beautiful Virginia home of the first Chief Justice of the U. S., reflects that good cheer and gracious dignity which made Southern hospitality famous. There is economy in its simplicity and cozy comfort within its well built walls.

Living and dining rooms fill one side of the house, with bay window toward garden. A well ventilated kitchen, with direct access to all parts of the house, is out of sight from living room. Windows light the stove and the sink, which is flanked by cabinets and broom closet. A side door connects yard, basement, and hall with closet which is adaptable for extra toilet. French doors open from living room to a spacious side porch.

Upstairs are bath, hall, four closets, two large and one smaller bedroom. Windows provide cross ventilation throughout the house and also light the dressing room off the front bedroom. For copies of the original drawings and floor plans, and the delivered price, fill out the Information Blank.

FIRST FLOOR PLAN

SECOND FLOOR PLAN

SEARS, ROEBUCK and CO.

The CLAREMONT Six Rooms and Bath

No. 3273—Honor Bilt Home.   Already Cut and Fitted

Monthly Payments as Low as $30 to $45

FLOOR PLAN

NO MATTER how much money a builder may have to invest in a home, he should aim at four objectives—appearance, convenience, durability and economy. In other words, he should make every dollar invested go as far as possible in securing a convenient, attractive home.

Americanized English style of architecture is expressed in the lines of this six-room bungalow. Exterior walls are stained shingles. The front entrance is unusual in design and forms a convenient vestibule and clothes closet.

THE SIZE of the plan is 24 ft. wide by 36 ft. deep with 9 ft. by 7 ft. 6 in. addition, which forms a grade and cellar entrance. The left side of the plan with entrance from the vestibule is devoted to the living room, dining room and kitchen. Note the convenient refrigerator platform in back entry. Bathroom is arranged so that all plumbing can be roughed in on one wall, saving on installation expense, and is planned to be equipped with built-in Venetian mirrored medicine case and Triple AAA quality plumbing

THIS HOME can also be furnished in five-room or seven-room arrangement.

Can be built on a 30-ft. lot.

For complete delivered price, fill out Information Blank enclosed.

The CRESTWOOD
Already Cut and Fitted—Standard Built Home
Monthly Payments as Low as $35 to $45

PLAN No. 3319 C size 24 ft. by 34 ft. 6 in. contains five rooms and bath, consisting of living room, dining room, kitchen and two bedrooms. A large combination living room and dining room size 12 ft. 5 in. by 22 ft. 11 in. can be formed by omitting the partition between these rooms. Can be built on a 30-ft. lot.

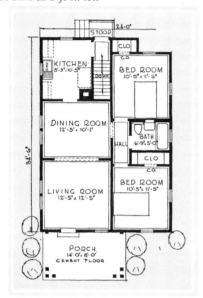

No. 3319-C

No. 3319-A

PLAN No. 3319-A four rooms and bath, size 22 ft. by 30 ft. with a 14-ft. by 8-ft. front porch. The large combination living and dining room is well lighted by three well proportioned windows. We have suggested location for kitchen sink, refrigerator, stove, cabinets and table. A complete home at a very low cost.

Fill out information blank and get complete delivered price, copy of original architectural elevations and floor plans.

PLAN No. 3319-D size 26 ft. wide by 38 ft. long contains three well arranged bedrooms, good size closets, living room, dining room and kitchen. No waste space in this plan which offers the maximum livable floor area at the lowest cost. Our famous "ready-cut" method saves hundreds of dollars.

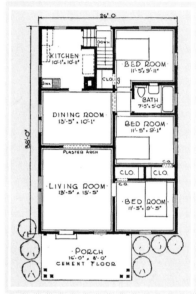

No. 3319-D

SEARS, ROEBUCK and CO.

The CRESCENT Five or Seven Rooms and Bath
3258-A—Already Cut and Fitted — 3259-A—Already Cut and Fitted
Monthly Payments as Low as $35 to $50

This well balanced bungalow with handsome Colonial entrance offers a choice of two floor plans, either of which would fit a 40-foot lot.

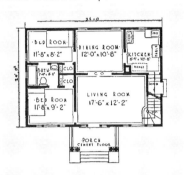

FLOOR PLAN 3258-A

PLAN 3258-A. Five rooms with pretty open stairway and space for finishing two rooms upstairs if desired. Two bedrooms and bath, two closets, kitchen cabinets and grade entrance. Size 34 ft. by 24 ft. with basement. First floor ceilings 9 ft. high. Living room 17 ft. 6 in. by 12 ft. 2 in. Convenient kitchen.

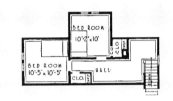

SECOND FLOOR PLAN 3258-A OPTION

PLAN 3259-A. Five rooms and two porches. Size 34 ft. by 26 ft. with a 20 ft. by 10 ft. addition. All rooms are larger than in 3258A with more windows, closets and cabinets. Stair, extra closet and all rooms open off hall except dining room. Inside and outside cellar entrances.

The living room is 20 ft. 3 in. by 12 ft. 3 in. with four large windows and good wall space. A semi-open stair from hall permits finishing off two additional bedrooms with closets on the second floor, if desired. The rear porch can be inexpensively screened and all rooms have cross ventilation. The kitchen cannot be

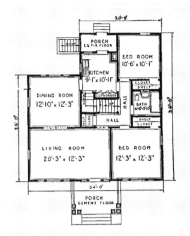

FLOOR PLAN 3259-A

seen from living room. Bedrooms and bath have complete privacy. First floor ceilings 9 ft. high. Basement, 7 ft. from floor to joists.

Fill out Information Blank for complete delivered price on material on either house and a copy of the architectural elevations and floor plans.

The RODESSA Four Rooms and Bath

RODESSA—FLOOR PLAN

IT IS HARDLY necessary to say that the Rodessa is a most attractive little home. The illustration proves it beyond a doubt. The price is also attractive. Much thought and expert advice have been employed in designing an exterior that will make this bungalow appeal to lovers of artistic homes. The interior plan appeals to those desiring the utmost economy in space.

THE RODESSA has proved to be one of our most popular houses, and owners are delighted with it. If you have only a moderate amount to invest, and wish to secure the biggest value for your money, with the greatest results in comfort, convenience and attractiveness, you can make no mistake in purchasing this home.

Size of plan is 22 ft. wide and 28 ft. long. Can be built on a lot 30 feet wide.

The GALEWOOD Five Rooms and Bath
No. 3294—Modern Home
Monthly Payments as Low as $35 to $45

FOR CONVENIENCE and economy it would be hard to beat this substantial and home-like brick bungalow.

The Living Room, with front and side windows, is 12 ft. 3 in. by 14 ft. 8 in. A plastered arch connects it with dining room. If desired, the partition between these rooms can be omitted, making one large room 12 ft. 3 in. wide and 25 ft. 3 in. long, using our Fold-Away breakfast furniture in the wall next to the kitchen, or a dropleaf table. A small hall off the dining room connects the well arranged bath with two bedrooms, each having cross ventilation and a large closet.

Fill out Information Blank for complete delivered price on either house, drawings and floor plans.

GALEWOOD—FLOOR PLAN

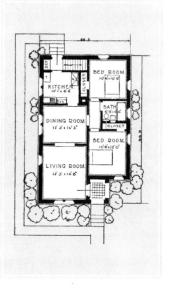

The STARLIGHT Five Rooms and Bath

No. 3307 — Modern Home — Already Cut and Fitted

Monthly Payments as Low as $25 to $40

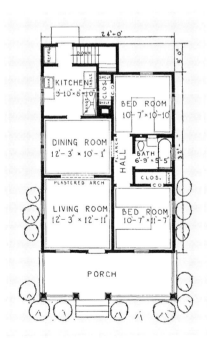

FLOOR PLAN

THE AVERAGE FAMILY purchases only one home in a life-time and naturally is interested in securing high quality materials backed by responsible service. All Honor Bilt Modern Homes are testimonials to our ability to serve with the building of your home.

This homelike five-room bungalow with its eleven cottage windows and big hospitable porch, its sturdy construction and high class materials, is planned for the family of average size. The Starlight does more than offer the largest possible rooms for its size. It offers the comfort of good arrangement, the orderliness of good closet space, construction such as we put in our finest homes, and quality which insures years of satisfaction.

THE WIDTH of the home is 24 feet—the length 37 feet and a 24-ft. by 8-ft. front porch. It can be built on a 30-ft. lot.

Picture the Starlight set among trees and shrubs; its walls painted white or ivory with green or red roof. It makes an attractive American cottage.

THE LEFT SIDE of the plan is devoted to living room, dining room, kitchen and combination grade and cellar entrance with refrigerator platform. The bedrooms and bath are connected by a small hall giving necessary privacy. Good wall space, large closets and plenty of windows are other noteworthy features.

Fill out Information Blank enclosed, for complete delivered price, outline of specifications and copies of the original ⅛-inch architectural drawings.

THE OAKDALE FLOOR PLAN

The OAKDALE Five Rooms and Bath
No. 3314—Honor Bilt Home
Monthly Payments as Low as $35 to $45

THIS pretty and home-like bungalow has a side entrance, centrally located kitchen, and a hall at the back from which bedrooms, bath and linen closet open. Quiet, privacy, and cross ventilation are thus assured for sleeping quarters and many steps saved the housewife.

The house is 24 ft. by 40 ft. with a 2-ft. extension for dining room. The porch is 16 ft. by 8 ft. There are five closets, clothes chute, fireplace, refrigerator niche and cabinets. Wonderfully convenient. Fill out Information Blank for delivered price and large drawings.

The FAIRY Four Rooms and Bath
No. 3316—Modern Home
Monthly Payments as Low as $25 to $30

THE charming simplicity of this soft stained shingled bungalow with combined living and dining room, makes it very economical. Fold-away breakfast furniture can be built in if desired. One bedroom and bath open off hall, the other opens off the living room. There are two closets, two cabinets and a grade entrance with space for refrigerator. Kitchen has two windows and space for stove near chimney. House is 22 ft. by 28 ft. and fits a 30-ft. lot. Fill out Information Blank for delivered price of all material and copy of architect's drawings.

THE FAIRY FLOOR PLAN

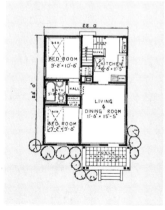

The VALLONIA Five or Eight Rooms

No. 13049A—5 Rooms.   No. 13049B—8 Rooms
Monthly Payments as Low as $35 to $50

THE VALLONIA is a prize bungalow home judging from the photographs and letters which hundreds of satisfied owners have written us, telling of their delight in its splendid features and wonderful value. It has an overhanging roof with timber cornice effect and shingled dormer with three windows. Sided with Cypress (the wood eternal). Porch extends across the front of the house, with lattice beneath.

FIRST FLOOR: The living and dining room, both

SECOND FLOOR PLAN

FIRST FLOOR PLAN

large, well proportioned rooms with good wall space and plenty of light, are connected by wide cased opening. A swinging door opens into a pleasant kitchen with ample space for table and chairs. Four windows light the kitchen and convenient pantry. Refrigerator space is in vestibule near grade entrance. A hall containing two closets gives privacy to the two bedrooms and bath. Each bedroom has a closet and two windows giving cross ventilation. The bathroom has Venetian mirrored medicine case and modern fixtures.

SECOND FLOOR: In the five-room house No. 13049, a closed stairway with a door from the dining room leads to the large attic. In Plan 13049B, which has eight rooms, an open stairway from the dining room leads to two large bedrooms, a smaller room in which additional plumbing could be installed if wanted, and three big closets.

Fill in Information Blank and we will send price and large architect's drawing with floor plans.

The HAWTHORNE Six Rooms and Bath

No. 3311—Honor Bilt Home
Monthly Payments as Low as $45 to $60

The HAWTHORNE fits modern conditions by turning the living and dining rooms toward the garden and building a garden porch under the main roof. The side entrance prevents tradesmen from intruding. With kitchen in front, the housewife can keep an eye on things and reach either front or back door in a few steps. The house is 30 ft. wide and 26 ft. deep, covered with 24-inch clear Red Cedar Royal Shingles. A compact, comfortable, and up-to-date Colonial home at a real saving.

FIRST FLOOR at left: Fireplace, French door, plaster arches, vestibule, and large hall closet, make the living room pleasant. The large dining room, like all other rooms, has windows on two sides and good wall spaces. Cabinets are beside the sink and above the refrigerator space, broom closet nearest to the hall.

SECOND FLOOR: Three large bedrooms, four closets and a well planned bath with recessed tub and Venetian mirrored wall cabinet, open off hall. Fill out Information Blank for price, drawings and floor plans.

The HAMMOND Five Rooms and Bath

No. 3347—Modern Home
Monthly Payments as Low as $40 to $50

In the HAMMOND we present the always popular five-room bungalow in a new guise, up-to-date outside and in, with beauty and distinction seldom found in houses of this size and remarkably low cost. In sturdy "Honor Bilt" construction, with high quality guaranteed materials, it will make the finest kind of an investment.

The main walls are to be covered with brick and the gables with wide siding. Dark face brick with stained siding would be attractive, but common brick whitewashed and white painted gables would be just as beautiful. There is always a fascination in a house with interesting details, such as the massive chimney of the HAMMOND with its clay pots, the triple windows which give such promise of a lovely living room, and the unique entrance. This is a house which will stand out among its neighbors and be a great source of pride to its fortunate owners.

FLOOR PLAN: The front vestibule and coat closet are lighted by a casement sash. Another closet is tucked into the corner of the large living room, which is 20 ft. by 11 ft. 6 in. An attractive fireplace, and windows grouped on two walls make this a delightful room. The kitchen is out of sight, only the dining room with its double windows being visible. The kitchen, with cross ventilation and convenient grade entrance, has cabinets grouped around the sink and the window above it. The side entrance is convenient for drive and saves garden space in back.

A hall to the right of living room leads to bath, linen closet, and two good sized corner bedrooms, each having

a closet, windows on two sides, and good wall space. Ceiling height on the first floor is 8 ft. 6 in. The basement is 7 feet from floor to joists. The house is 34 ft. 11 in. wide and 31 ft. 5 in. deep on the bedroom side. It can be built on a lot 41 feet or more in width, but requires 45 feet with side drive.

Fill out the Information Blank and we will send you complete delivered price on the material, which is all fully guaranteed, and a copy of the original architectural drawings and floor plans.

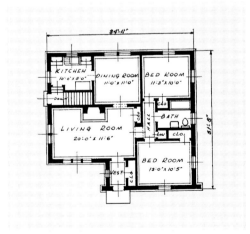

FLOOR PLAN

The WORCHESTER Six Rooms and Bath

No. 3291—Modern Home
Monthly Payments as Low as $55 to $70

A well built brick home of such simple dignity, beauty and economy as the WORCHESTER, makes a wonderful investment. The style will always be good and bring profitable rental or selling price. This house is 30 ft. 11 in. by 22 ft. 11 in. and could be built with a side drive on a lot 40 ft. wide. It has six comfortable corner rooms all with cross ventilation, five closets, bath, two vestibules, basement and an attic with stairs from one of the front bedrooms.

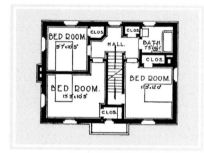

SECOND FLOOR PLAN

FIRST FLOOR: Facing the entrance are the pretty telephone cabinet and Colonial stair. Plastered arches open to the living room and dining room, both of which are at the front of the house, with ample windows and wall spaces. Opposite the fireplace in the long living room is a large recess for davenport. Cabinets surround the sink and the window above it. Broom closet, and space for refrigerator are in entry way.

SECOND FLOOR: Bath, linen closet and three bedrooms, each of which has windows on two sides and a closet, open off the hall. The well arranged bath, with Venetian cabinet, is at the back.

Fill out Information Blank and we will send price and large architect's drawings and floor plans.

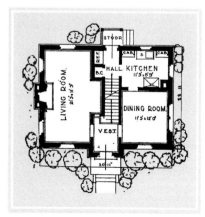

FIRST FLOOR PLAN

SEARS, ROEBUCK and CO.

The GORDON Five or Seven Rooms and Bath

No. 3356—Modern Home
Monthly Payments as Low as $45 to $60

THE SIMPLE dignity and beauty of Colonial architecture found many expressions, one of the most interesting being the Cape Cod Colonial, exemplified in the GORDON. Many of these sturdy houses still standing in New England, are objects of pilgrimage to those who appreciate and love beautiful homes. Although face brick is often used for the chimney, good effect is obtained by using common brick whitewashed.

The GORDON is a most adaptable plan, as the first floor constitutes a complete five room house, but two or

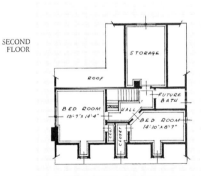

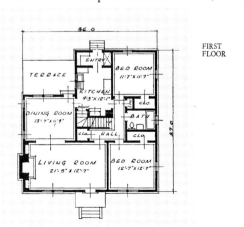

three additional rooms may be completed on the second floor whenever needed. One very good second floor arrangement here shown, affords two large bedrooms and closets, with an additional bathroom.

FIRST FLOOR at left: Central stairways, one above the other, lead to the basement and to the second floor. The stair hall which connects all rooms and bath, contains two extra closets. The two corner bedrooms have each a closet and windows on two sides. The large enclosed kitchen entry will suggest many uses. A fireplace, and a terrace reached from the dining room are other good features. SECOND FLOOR, plans above, contain extra sleeping quarters and large storage room.

The SOLACE Six Rooms and Bath

No. 3218—Modern Home—Already Cut and Fitted
Monthly Payments as Low as $30 to $45

THE SOLACE is a story and a half American Cottage type home, designed to give the maximum livable area at the lowest possible cost. The living room, dining room, one bedroom and bath on the first floor provide complete living accommodations for a small family.

SECOND FLOOR PLAN

SHOULD YOU DESIRE to do so, rooms on the second floor can be left to be finished later.

The Kitchen. Here a compact, convenient arrangement is suggested for location of range, sink, refrigerator and cabinets. One counter and two wall units are included, all Standard Equipment. A combination grade and cellar entrance is designed underneath the main stairs. Two large bedrooms will be found on the second floor, head room for the stairs being formed by dormer at the rear.

All the material for Honor Bilt homes is fully guaranteed as to quality and quantity. THE SOLACE can be built on a 30-ft. lot.

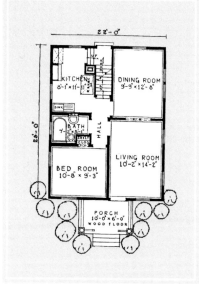

FIRST FLOOR PLAN

The KENDALE Six Rooms and Bath

No. 3298—Already Cut and Fitted Modern Home
Monthly Payments as Low as $40 to $50

CAN BE BUILT ON A 32-FOOT LOT

EXTERIOR. This Americanized English bungalow has exterior walls of face brick and stucco. The front entrance is unusual in design and its projection forms the convenient vestibule and closet.

INTERIOR. The Living Room and Dining Room are connected by an attractive plastered arch. Both rooms are well lighted and have plenty of wall space for convenient arrangement of all furniture. If desired, the partition between these rooms can be omitted, making one large room size 13 feet 2 inches wide and 24 feet 8 inches. Then we would suggest using our "Fold-away" breakfast furniture in the wall next to kitchen or drop leaf table.

The Kitchen is planned for efficient arrangement of range, table, etc. The rear entrance, cellar stairs and platform for refrigerator are located in the addition. Kitchen equipment includes one counter unit "H," one wall unit "J" and two wall units "D."

BEDROOMS AND BATH. A small hall separates the rear bedroom and bath from the dining room. Each of the two front bedrooms contain a good size closet.

The Basement is planned for heating plant, laundry, fuel room and storage.

Height of Ceilings. First floor 8 feet 6 inches, basement 7 feet from cellar floor to under side of joists.

Fill out Information Blank and we will send complete delivered price and a copy of the original drawings and floor plans.

FLOOR PLANS

The ELLISON Five or Seven Rooms and Bath

No. 3359—Modern Home
Monthly Payments as Low as $50 to $75

The ELLISON is another popular flexible bungalow type design which gives the prospective home builder the option of having five complete living rooms on the first floor and two additional rooms can be finished on the second floor when additional space is needed.

The exterior walls are planned to be covered with brick which we suggest finishing with whitewash and staining the porch columns and wood lintels dark brown. The home would look equally attractive if furnished in white stucco.

The first floor plan contains a large living room, story

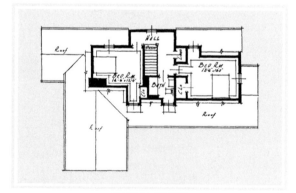

SECOND FLOOR

and a half type, with exposed ceiling beams, dining room and compact kitchen with convenient space for all modern equipment.

At the right of the main hall, a small passageway gives the two bedrooms and bath the necessary privacy, closet space for rear bedroom and has been provided with built-in wardrobe next to the bathroom.

In order that you will get a better picture of this very attractive home, we have prepared photostatic copies of the original architectural elevations and floor plans, copies of which will be sent to you together with Outline of Specifications, if you will fill out the Information Blank.

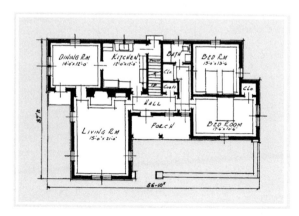

FIRST FLOOR

SEARS, ROEBUCK and CO.

The MILLERTON Six Rooms and Bath
No. 3358—Modern Home
Monthly Payments as Low as $60 to $75

This new type American design home is meeting with considerable popularity on account of the compact, efficient room arrangement, but gives a very serviceable arrangement at a minimum cost. The exterior is planned to be covered with brick which we suggest finishing with whitewash, leaving the coins at the corners with a red colored brick exposed.

An unusual feature is the right projection which con-

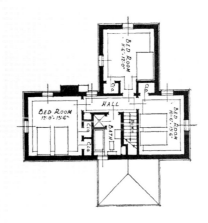

SECOND FLOOR PLAN

tains both the front and rear entrance—also has sufficient room to give two closets for outer wraps and lavatory.

All three rooms on the first floor are well lighted and contain exceptional wall space. Kitchen is compact and contains convenient space for all modern equipment. Three large bedrooms, five closets and bathroom with bathtub and shower stall complete the second floor plan.

Fill out Information Blank and we will send you complete delivered price on all material and a copy of the original architectural elevations and floor plans.

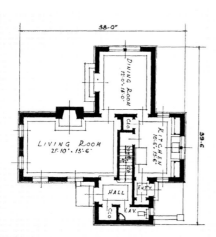

FIRST FLOOR PLAN

Index of Houses

Arranged by Number of Rooms

4 Rooms

Page
25 Hartford
27 Sunbury
34 Stanford
36 Wexford
37 Jeanette
38 Rochelle
41 Crafton
54 Ellsworth
66 Crestwood
68 Rodessa
70 Fairy

5 Rooms

Page
14 Willard
15 Lakecrest
18 Colchester
21 Berwyn
24 Mitchell
25 Hartford
31 Wheaton
33 Clifton
34 Stanford
35 Lewiston
36 Wexford
39 Stratford

Page
40 Jewel
41 Crafton
42 Bellewood
43 Westwood
45 Detroit
49 Winona
51 Collingwood
62 Randolph
63 Roxbury
66 Crestwood
67 Crescent
68 Galewood
69 Starlight
70 Oakdale
71 Vallonia
73 Hammond
75 Gordon
78 Ellison

6 Rooms

Page
13 Elmhurst
20 Dover
22 Lorain
23 Lynnhaven
26 Maplewood
41 Crafton

Page
46 Strathmore
47 Belmont
48 Mansfield
49 Winona
50 Brookwood
60 Gladstone
64 Richmond
65 Claremont
66 Crestwood
72 Hawthorne
74 Worchester
76 Solace
77 Kendale
79 Millerton

6 Rooms with Attached Garage

Page
12 Hillsboro

7 Rooms

Page
17 Lexington
33 Clifton
35 Lewiston
44 Norwich
52 Carroll

Page
58 Carrington
59 Kenfield
67 Crescent
75 Gordon
78 Ellison

7 Rooms with Attached Garage

Page
28 Torrington
56 Corning
57 Trenton

8 Rooms

Page
18 Colchester
19 New Haven
29 Jefferson
32 Oak Park
53 Birmingham
71 Vallonia

2-Apartment Houses — "Income Homes"

Page
55 Dexter
61 La Salle

Alphabetical List of Designs

Page
Bellewood............42
Belmont.............47
Berwyn..............21
Birmingham..........53
Brookwood...........50
Carrington..........58
Carroll.............52
Claremont...........65
Clifton.............33
Colchester..........18
Collingwood.........51
Corning.............56
Crafton.............41
Crescent............67
Crestwood...........66
Detroit.............45
Dexter..............55

Page
Dover...............20
Ellison.............78
Ellsworth...........54
Elmhurst............13
Fairy...............70
Galewood............68
Gladstone...........60
Gordon..............75
Hammond.............73
Hartford............25
Hawthorne...........72
Hillsboro...........12
Jeanette............37
Jefferson...........29
Jewel...............40
Kendale.............77
Kenfield............59

Page
Lakecrest...........15
LaSalle.............61
Lewiston............35
Lexington...........17
Lorain..............22
Lynnhaven...........23
Mansfield...........48
Maplewood...........26
Millerton...........79
Mitchell............24
New Haven...........19
Norwich.............44
Oakdale.............70
Oak Park............32
Randolph............62
Richmond............64
Rochelle............38

Page
Rodessa.............68
Roxbury.............63
Solace..............76
Stanford............34
Starlight...........69
Stratford...........39
Strathmore..........46
Sunbury.............27
Torrington..........28
Trenton.............57
Vallonia............71
Westwood............43
Wexford.............36
Wheaton.............31
Willard.............14
Winona..............49
Worchester..........74

Sears, Roebuck and Co. Offer a Complete Construction Service

THEY BUILD and finance your home regardless of whether it contains four rooms or forty.

The lot on which you plan to build may be irregular in size, or your room requirements and personal taste may be just a little different. If you already have a plan of your own or have accumulated a number of sketches and ideas from magazines, we suggest that you send them to us and let us study the details and give you the benefit of our wonderful purchasing power and Finance Plan.

IF YOU HAVE NOT had special plans drawn up but have a fairly definite idea as to the number of rooms, size, arrangement, etc. that you require, attach a rough sketch of your ideas to the Questionnaire in back of this book, giving us all other necessary information that will guide us in helping you select your home. Our staff of experts is at your disposal to serve you in accordance with your ideas.

ON THIS PAGE we have illustrated the original architectural pen and ink rendering of our Modern Home the "Hillsboro." We have also shown an actual photograph of how this attractive English bungalow type home appears when completed. Note how every detail has been carried out by the contractor.

WE MAINTAIN for your convenience, a complete service department enabling you to secure preliminary sketches incorporating your own personal desires and our recommendations as to the most economical way to build your home particularly with the use of our stock millwork details and best of materials purchased in quantity, at great saving to you. These preliminary plans consist of two

elevations and floor plans drawn to $\frac{1}{8}$ inch scale, and contain sufficient detail to give you a very definite idea of the exterior appearance and the interior arrangement of your proposed new home. They also enable us to work up complete material and construction cost for you so that you will know exactly what your home is going to cost complete before any other expense is involved.

LET the World's Largest Builders of Fine Homes assist you in getting the exact home you want at the lowest possible cost. We are prepared to cooperate with the best local architects doing residential work in each local community.

PLAN AND BUILD NOW to get the benefit of present low prices on materials and construction.

AT THE RIGHT we illustrate the method in which the $\frac{1}{8}$-inch preliminary elevations are prepared, and above is an actual photograph showing how the home looked when complete.

FILL OUT the Questionnaire with information about your proposed new home and we will send you a complete folder containing $\frac{1}{8}$-inch floor plans, two elevations, large scale illustrations of plumbing and lighting fixtures, also detailed outline of the material and equipment we recommend for your home.